Living

in the

Golden Light

HEALING WITH THE GOLDEN ANGELS OF THE FIVE
ELEMENTS AND THE GOLDEN LIGHT PLANT ESSENCES.

Pati Solva Hueneke

BALBOA
PRESS

Balboa Press books may be ordered through booksellers or by contacting:

Balboa Press
A Division of Hay House
1663 Liberty Drive
Bloomington, IN 47403
www.balboapress.com
1-(877) 407-4847

www.goldenlightessences.com
or contact the author at 2 Lambell Close, Palmerston ACT
2913, Australia. Email phueneke@bigpond.com

Because of the dynamic nature of the Internet, any Web addresses or links contained in this book may have changed since publication and may no longer be valid. The views expressed in this work are solely those of the author and do not necessarily reflect the views of the publisher, and the publisher hereby disclaims any responsibility for them.

ISBN: 978-1-4525-0069-0 (sc)
ISBN: 978-1-4525-0071-3 (dj)
ISBN: 978-1-4525-0070-6 (e)

Library of Congress Control Number: 2010914870

The author of this book does not dispense medical advice or prescribe the use of any technique as a form of treatment for physical, emotional, or medical problems without the advice of a physician, either directly or indirectly. The intent of the author is only to offer information of a general nature to help you in your quest for emotional and spiritual well-being. In the event you use any of the information in this book for yourself, which is your constitutional right, the author and the publisher assume no responsibility for your actions.

Any people depicted in stock imagery provided by Thinkstock are models, and such images are being used for illustrative purposes only.
Certain stock imagery © Thinkstock.

Printed in the United States of America
Balboa Press rev. date:11/12/2010

For my beloved Gurumayi who gave me the great gift of Grace - the recognition that we are indeed the Divine Golden Light of Consciousness of All.

About the Author

Pati Solva Hueneke is a herbalist, iridologist, pranic and spiritual healer, psychic healing medium, ayurvedic lifestyle consultant, siddha yogi, angel healer, author and teacher who works from her Golden Light Healing Clinic in Palmerston, Canberra, Australia. Pati developed the Golden Light Plant Healing Essences from her 17 years of experience with herbal healing after a profound mystical yogic experience of the materialization of the Divine inner Golden Light Being.

The 36 Golden Light Plant Healing Essences have been created and manufactured by Pati using many organic herbs and flowers from her garden in Palmerston and offer emotional, spiritual and physical healing by allowing us to release negative energy patterns as we surrender more and more to the Golden Divine Light of our own inner true nature.

Pati offers seminars from her clinic and anywhere in the world as guided by Spirit, to attune others to a more refined experience of this Golden Divine Light and to explore the healing powers of the plant kingdom of Mother Earth through the essences. She also offers personal healing consultations using herbs and essences as well as pranic and spiritual healing either privately or online.

You can contact Pati at www.goldenlightessences.com (her online shop) and at phueneke@bigpond.com or write to her at:

The Golden Light Healing Clinic,
2 Lambell Close,
Palmerston , A.C.T., 2913 ,
Australia.

"The gold that emanates from the Divine person wants to penetrate into humanity..."

-Hildegard of Bingen (1098-1179)

Preface

I am delighted to present **Living in the Golden Light** *to you, which includes the* **Golden Light Essences and Meditations***. This book and these essences have taken quite a while to see the light of day; seventeen years in fact. Seventeen years of clinical practice and twenty years of meditation and spiritual healing practices have made all this possible. The 36 vibrational healing plant essences – The Golden Light Essences – were developed in my herbal and spiritual healing practice in Palmerston, ACT, Australia- a small "Findhorn" right here in Canberra! Using plant and flower tinctures which I have made myself, many of which come from my own organic garden, I have been able to distil the alchemical gold from the plant tinctures and infuse it into the concentrated stock to produce these profound healing essences. In deep meditation I received the "knowing" that these essences vibrate to the number five and to the fifth dimension of healing, to the element of gold and the Vedic sun signs. The five Golden Angels of the Elements have graced me with the knowledge of their healing secrets and Mother Earth has also come to the party.*

On the 17th of August, 2003, after 13 years of following my spiritual path of Siddha Yoga meditation, I had a profound mystical experience of awakening which led to my spending one month in my meditation master's ashram. There I was given the great good fortune of seeing my own Divine inner Golden Light Being- my inner great Self and the Self of All, materialize before me. What amazing grace and what a beautiful gift my beloved meditation master and Guru bestowed upon me. This changed my life in every way. I had an experience of knowing who I really was and what each one of us carries within us – our own inner Divinity – our own inner Golden sun which illuminates everyone and everything.

I brought this experience back to my clinical healing work and in meditation 36 healing plant essences were revealed to me. Their healing properties, method of manufacture and how to prescribe them were also made known to me. They have been infused with Golden Light energy for healing in a deep and safe way which neutralizes personal Karma and brings you into your positive sun energy.

Over the next seven years, I taught about them in my clinic and at Health Schools Australia seminars and used them in my clinic with great results. I held workshops on them from 2007 to 2009 which included making them and conducting guided healing meditations on each of the 36 plant essences. My niece and her father, Angie and Jim Matsinos, both artists with a deep interest in herbal healing, helped me develop the 36 Golden Light Essence divinatory card deck. The cards in this deck can be used to choose a healing essence for whole zodiac healing or for healing a specific issue. This healing will bring you even further into living in your own Golden Divine Light.

My students and patients gave me great feedback and I thank them with all my heart for their confidence and trust in me as a healer.

*So here are **Living in the Golden Light** and the **Golden Light Essences**. I hope they can be of great healing benefit to you and allow you to live in the experience of YOUR own inner Divine Golden Light.*

Please send me feedback on your unique healing experiences of these essences. I give them to you with Great Love - enjoy as you move into the new Golden Age of Living here on Golden Mother Earth.

With Love and Golden Light Angel healing Blessings to ALL,
from
Pati Solva Hueneke,
Canberra/Australia, August, 17th, 2010.

Dedication

To all the divine herbal healers, to my teachers, mentors, and all my beloved patients – thank you for all the knowledge and wisdom you have imparted to me in my life's work of healing.

Invocation

Divine spiritual guides, healers, teachers and Ascended Masters; healing Angels and Archangels Gabriel and Raphael; my beloved Guru and all the Siddhas; my herbal healing and Ayurvedic teachers; Divine Pranic healers and teachers; the Tibetan Blue Medicine Buddha; White Eagle; the Golden Christos Sun energy; the Divine Mother and Moon energy; Mother Earth; the 5 Golden Angels of the Elements and Karma, I humbly ask you for your continued blessings in my life's calling of herbal and spiritual healing work. Blessings to all the readers of this book. Thank you. In full faith. So be it and so it is!

Pati Solva Hueneke
17th of August, 2010

Contents

The 36 Golden Light Essences

1. Alfalfa
2. Burdock
3. Chamomile
4. Comfrey
5. Damask Rose
6. Elderflower
7. Fenugreek
8. Gardenia
9. Gentian
10. Golden Seal
11. Hops
12. Hypericum
13. Hyssop
14. Iris
15. Kelp
16. Lavender
17. Lemon Balm
18. Lotus
19. Mary's Thistle
20. Meadowsweet
21. Mistletoe
22. Mugwort
23. Oats
24. Passionflower
25. Peony
26. Plantain
27. Red Clover
28. Rosemary
29. Sarsparilla
30. Skullcap
31. Sunflower
32. Valerian
33. Vervain
34. Violet
35. Yarrow
36. Yellow Dock

Chapter 1.   What is the Golden Light?

The Golden Light is Universal Intelligence which is projected into our world from within the Silence of Oneness. It permeates all of life and lives within this Great Silence where it can be contacted through deep meditation (especially when in the theta state) and being in a space of purity of heart and love. Embracing ourselves with unconditional love, compassion and forgiveness is one way of connecting with this Golden Light.

We are all surrounded by the Golden Light which can be "seen" as the outermost layer of our subtle body in our aura. Within this "ketheric" layer of our aura is our link to our eternal soul and to our Akashic records. These are a complete cosmic record of our individual soul's existence in all dimensions of space and time. The "ketheric" layer interpenetrates all the other layers including the physical body. Connecting with, healing and strengthening this aura of golden light can enable us to feel very protected and supported in all that we do here on Earth. It enhances our immune systems and brings us into line with our agreed Divine Life Purpose in this incarnation. It gives us the opportunity to take back our own God-given Divine power and use it in service for the good of all. It offers us the possibility of discovering how the Sun's light interacts and participates with our own inner sun in our soul journey here on Earth and in the other dimensions of life. The Golden Light is free and it is available to all. It assists us on our evolutionary journey of expanding consciousness.

The Golden Divine Light is within YOU. It also resides in the inner cave of your own heart chakra. Spirit permeates Golden Light with the heartfelt sensation of unconditional love. It is the essential spark of life living in the secret fifth chamber in the inner cave of the heart. It is the God and Goddess energy which may whisper silently to us and touches our heart with gratitude and love for all of life. It belongs to you and to everyone. It is our human birthright. When you have the intention and give your permission, you can awaken to this Divinity with the assistance, protection and blessings of the Five Golden Angels of the purified and balanced elements of the Christos Sun energy (the Divine Spiritual Sun behind the physical sun). They will carry your intent through the beams of the Golden Light to support you with their Love. They will assist you in transforming the energy of fear and lack into love and abundance. This Golden Sun energy enters through the crown chakra to the pineal gland which acts like a prism to break down the information into seven colour-coded ray bands and guides them to the appropriate energy centres in the body to nourish us on all levels. The pineal gland also acts as a bridge to connect the right and left hemispheres of the brain; the yin and the yang; the feminine and the masculine; the negative and the positive, into the union - the sacred marriage of the opposites. This experience of oneness, of unity with all that is, may be felt as a deep knowing of the truth, as intuitive feeling and rational thinking are united.

The healing information carried in this Golden Light can assist you in releasing crystallized energy from your karmic timeline which is no longer of use to you and indeed may be appearing as disease and pain at this time. You will experience more health, happiness, peace, human love and abundance in your life here on Earth as you release old outworn ideas about yourself and remember more fully who you really are and who we all are in truth - Divine Beings of the Golden Light of Love. You will step out of the third dimension of duality and polarity consciousness into the fifth dimension of Love, Joy and Bliss whilst staying in your physical body here on Earth. This is a very personal experience even though it is also planetary and cosmic.

First you may experience the unified thought field of "I AM ONE with ALL THAT IS" when all your chakras are awakened, balanced and unified. There are ways of doing this, through meditation, pranic healing, Reiki, crystals, healing plant essences, sound healing (OM) and spontaneously through a descent of Divine Grace. Many of us are experiencing some of this at this point in time. The awakening to the Golden Divine Light within your own heart can follow this chakra unification. The key is TRUST. Trust in your own inner Divine Golden Self - surrender to the spiritual Golden Light in your very own heart and in the heart of all beings. Trust, that everything in your life is in Divine Order right NOW, even though you may have doubts about it sometimes.

The five Golden Light Angels of the harmonized Elements welcome everyone. They do not judge. They see this Golden Light in every human heart and in all of Creation. Trust is the gateway to this Divine awakening and as this trust centre grows in energy, you can experience a certainty about your own inner knowing and senses of inner sight, hearing, touch and feeling. These "gifts" can help you and protect you in your daily life here on Earth and bring you into the "right relationship" with people around you. They can also give you the insights you need to lead a peaceful, healthy and abundant life right here and now.

What are some of the gifts of this Divine Awakening? Firstly, there is less polarity within the duality, i.e. the swings are smaller, the crises and dramas are less. There is a greater sense of balance, choices and pathways become clearer, feelings of being loved and supported increase. You "see" these more clearly. You feel more love for yourself. You find it easier to stay positive about life and your daily experiences. You start to see the good in more situations even though once you may have thought you couldn't, or that some things in your life were a complete disaster. You learn the positive life lessons from these experiences more easily and quickly. You have a greater sense of overall well-being, less doubt and internal questioning of what is right and wrong, and more answers. You feel less lost and fragmented; more whole. You can focus less on so called "problems" and more on the solutions to those perceived "problems", and more quickly. You become more creative, empowered, invigorated and in control of your life instead of reacting to events, feelings and people. You feel less stress and more BLISS! These gifts of living in the fifth dimension become more anchored in this third dimension here on Earth, now. You become aware of the ever expanding nature of Consciousness and the part that you play in this Divine Play.

You are the centre of the Sun. Your Golden Light radiates from within to everyone and everything. Let this Golden Light expand!

Your inner sun is the closest you can get to the experience of your own Being, your Divine flame in this Earth plane. It is your source of inexhaustible energy from within your own self and connected to the spiritual Sun beyond the psychical sun. The more you relax into just Being, the more you connect with this infinite source of sun energy within your own self. As you relax, you start to let go of negative emotions and thoughts more and more and experience positive ones which allow you to see solutions to so called "problems" in your life. You start to experience yourself as being connected to the ONE of all of creation and your outer circumstances improve and suffering eases as this process takes place within you, around you. Meditating in the "Great Silence" - the Source of all Creation, can also bring you to the centre of your sun.

The Golden Light surrounds everyone as the outermost layer of the subtle bodies of your aura. You are enclosed in the Golden Light as in a sphere. This is our interface with the divinity of all that is. We can and do experience this divine connection to our own "God within" quite often, even if we are not fully conscious of it; such as in "aha" moments, flashes of intuition and knowing, synchronicities or so-called "coincidences "in our lives, meetings with just the right people at just the right time, meeting the "love of our life" and much more. In deep meditation when we surrender to the "Great Silence", the source of all, we may connect directly with this Golden Light energy. All the subtle bodies of the aura are contained within this Golden Light.

Here is a "play" that can connect you more with this Golden Divine Light in your own heart.

The Golden Cross with the Divine Rose at the centre

Note: These 3 diagrams can be coloured a golden yellow to connect you with the Golden Light Energy.

The Golden Cross represents the four elements in humanity and the natural world. At the centre is the Divine Rose, the fifth element of the Divine Ether - the breath of God. The five subtle bodies are infused with the energy of the five elements and the five Golden Angels of Karma can help to purify them.

The physical subtle body is supported by the earth element.
The emotional subtle body is supported by the water element.
The mental subtle body is supported by the air element.
The energetic subtle body is supported by the fire element.
The spiritual subtle body is supported by the ether element.

Gaze at the Golden Cross and the Divine Heart of the golden rose at its centre as you connect with your breath and meditate for a while, invoking the assistance of the five Golden Angels of the Elements and Healing as they purify, restore and balance all five bodies and elements. Come back to the here and now, feeling light, but very grounded. How does this feel for you?

May you continue to experience grace-filled healing powers of the Divine Golden Light in your life as you move into living in the Fifth Dimension here on Mother Earth. We can all move into this Fifth Dimension with Mother Earth who is also changing and moving with us. Feel the Golden Light washing over you like a shower of rain. Feel the joy of the recognition of your own Golden Divine Self.

Chapter 2. My personal path to the awakening of the Golden Light

Let me share some highlights of my personal experience of the awakening of the Golden Light with you now.

During the year of 2003, at the age of 52, I had the good fortune of being able to make a pilgrimage to my meditation teacher's ashram in South Fallsburg in the beautiful Catskill Mountains in upstate New York, USA.

I have been practicing Siddha Yoga meditation since 1990 and received "Shaktipat" or spiritual awakening from my beloved teacher, Gurumayi, in late September of that year at a meditation intensive. I experienced the greatest flooding of Divine love in my heart and whole being, which changed my perspective on life completely. I am not the same person I was before that experience. I awoke from a deep sleep of forgetfulness of my own true loving nature. My eyes were pierced with Divine rays of light, from which I could not protect myself. This Divine light of pure love entered my heart and filled it up to bursting point. An energy stirred at the base of my spine and soared up the inner channel to the crown of my head which lifted up like a vault and then a great light spilled over my entire being. What bliss, what ecstasy. I was being drowned in Divine love. I asked spontaneously to be given ways of sharing this great love with others, as I couldn't contain it in my own being.

Soon after I met my second husband, who is also a Siddha Yogi and we have continued to meditate and follow this spiritual and life path together.

I have been working in my herbal healing practice for the last 18 years and have continued with my meditation and Siddha Yoga practices which are still bringing me great healing blessings and sustain me with inner strength on this somewhat tricky Earth walk of mine. The memory of the great Divine love within me, which I see in everyone, is still with me. I also see this Divine light of love in all the plants and herbs I use in my healing practice. This is the energy of true healing. It is the Alchemy of transformation from forgetfulness to remembrance of the Divine Self, which is present in everyone and everything. I love to remember this experience each moment of each day and it truly sustains me through my life.

After many years of meditation, meeting my beloved teacher here in Canberra in April of 1991 and in Auckland in May of the same year and attending many intensives and retreats, on 17th of August , 2003, I attended another Siddha Yoga meditation intensive here in Canberra. The theme of the intensive was to be resolute in trusting the Great Self within. I fell into a deep meditation and suddenly all my spiritual energy centres or chakras along my subtle spine started spinning at a great speed and exploded in a great fireworks display of light. My heart was filled with starlight and also exploded. I was given the inner message by my Guru, "You are Pati-pat Shiva. All wandering has ended. You are one with the All of the Universe. Blessings to you dear one." My heart was filled with gratitude for I felt so loved and so fortunate. I was going "home" while still in my physical body. My great yearning to know God in this lifetime was being granted to me. This yearning had been with me since my early childhood.

God appeared to me as the great Light of my very own Self and the awareness dawned on me that this is also the Light in everyone and everything. I now felt a great yearning to serve my beloved meditation teacher and to spend time with her. I really didn't know how this would happen but sent out the wish to the universe, "Bring me to Gurumayi soon, please!"

A few weeks later, my dear husband, Klaus suggested we could use some of our savings for my trip to see Gurumayi who was at the Siddha Yoga Ashram in upstate New York, South Fallsburg in the Catskill Mountains. I arranged a new passport, wrote to the Ashram to see if I could visit and do 'seva' (service) there, organized my airfares and everything went very smoothly. On the 1st of October, 2003 I was on the way to seeing my beloved Gurumayi for the whole month of October. What excitement!

After a rather long flight via Tokyo, I arrived at the Ashram a few days later. It was autumn there. Sleet was falling and it was already quite cold, but I didn't feel at all cold, as I was literally "burning" in the fire of Yoga. I wore little red shoes, without socks or stockings and felt like Dorothy in the Wizard of OZ travelling to a new land of mystical wonder. The Ashram is also on Brickman Road which reminded me of the Yellow Brick Road that Dorothy travels along in the story. I felt so exhilarated and energized. When I arrived there, I went straight to the Nityananda temple to give thanks to all the Siddhas for the incredible Grace that had been given to me. And the Grace kept coming and coming and coming. This feeling of being surrounded by Divine Grace was, and still is with me constantly. I settled in and was given the "Seva" (selfless service) of working in the kitchen cutting up vegetables. At first I was quite taken aback with this work, but as I surrendered to the task and focused on it, an incredible feeling of peace came over me. Everywhere I went in the ashram, it was saturated with this Grace, this Divine Peace and Serenity. It felt like Heaven on Earth. Whenever I thought of something I needed or wanted to know, a person would "magically" appear, giving me the information or helping me with something. I saw my beloved Gurumayi quite often in the temple and felt so at one with her. Inner messages of love and support flooded into my consciousness there. Each day I walked about two kilometres along the "silent path" to the kitchens where I did my seva and met the most amazing people from all over the world. Many of them thought that my 'Aussie' way of speaking and thinking was quite amusing and there was a lot of joy and laughter. The food tasted great and I never had one single stomach pain (as I often had at home). What a truly divine experience. I had the deepest meditation experiences in the silent cave every day, attended chanting and special celebrations. I was truly in Heaven.

At the end of October there was a large celebration and Meditation Intensive and a few thousand people were expected to attend. So the work in the kitchen was full on. I managed to leave at 5pm on the evening before the Intensive, as Gurumayi was giving me the inner message that I needed to rest and take care of myself. I was to see myself nurtured like a little baby before I attended the Intensive. There was so much work to be done and the people in the kitchen did not want me to leave. I agonized over this. I finally decided that I had to follow my inner guidance and look after myself, so I left at 5pm, feeling very guilty. As I left, five more people entered the kitchen saying, "Can we help?" Oh the workings of Grace! I learnt a big lesson that day. It is always my little self or ego that makes me think that I am the only one who can do something. As soon as I let go, everything fell into place and help came.

The meditation intensive weekend arrived and as I was in deep meditation, I was again bathed in Grace. Gurumayi spoke about surrender - the sweet surrender in strength, to our own inner divinity, to the golden flame within our own hearts. I felt a deep trust and relaxation come over me. I felt so completely loved and supported. Quite spontaneously, I had a vision of Gurumayi and her Guru, Baba Muktananda, merging into the great red, pulsating Heart of Jesus. Mother Mary was also there. All these Great Ones merged into one. Suddenly, out of my face, emerged a beautiful golden light being. It stood before me. In wonderment, I asked, "who are you?" I received the answer, "I am you of course". My whole body started shaking uncontrollably. Luckily a person called Sheila (looking after us in the hall) came to me to help ground me. She comforted me and gave me a banana to eat. I was so overcome with intense emotions.

It took some time for me to return to normal consciousness. I was in total awe of my experience. I was spellbound. I was totally amazed. What did this mean? Yes, I am the Golden Light of consciousness! The awareness came to me that this is who we all are in truth. This inner golden Treasure is within us all, just waiting to be recognised and released. I felt totally loved, totally relaxed and free of any tension, at one with all of life, everyone and everything. All things seemed possible again. An incredible energy surged up my spine and into every cell of my being. I knew that I had finally caught a "glimpse of God" while still in my physical body. "God" was within me and part of me. The greatest good fortune had descended upon me. I was "home". I had no idea what would happen to me in my life from then on, but I had regained the trust that it could only be good, no matter what it was. A lot of fear left me, especially any fear of God that I had felt in the past. I felt worthy of this experience and realised that the greatest trick the little ego has, is to try to convince us that we are not worthy of knowing and experiencing our own great Golden Light of Divinity.

The next day was the "Festival of Lights" at the Ashram and there were candles everywhere. The whole Ashram was bathed in LIGHT. I experienced a beautiful healing massage at a spa retreat near the Ashram. I was floating in bliss.

Soon I returned home and that Golden Light feeling just seemed to grow and grow in me every time I remembered it. Eventually I was able to ground this energy in developing the Golden Light Plant Essences and connecting with the Golden Angels of Healing.

I am forever deeply grateful to Gurumayi and all the Siddhas for showing me the truth of what I really am and who we all are - the Golden Light of Divine Consciousness. I continue to experience this Golden Light in new ways in my meditations and everyday life. I often feel spontaneous joy and happiness arise within me, seemingly for no reason. I hope I can share some of this Golden Light with you, my readers, as we continue to journey together on this path of finding our way back to our own true golden natures as human beings living here in harmony on Mother Earth.

So let me guide you in a meditation on this Golden Light and see what you experience. Let's go on an adventure of discovery with the Golden Light and the Golden Angels of the five Elements!

Chapter 3. A healing guided meditation

Below is a healing guided meditation to reconnect you to the Golden Light Angels of the Elements and your own inner Golden Light Body. Enjoy!

As you read this guided meditation it WILL take you to your own inner Golden Light. You will experience its healing power directly as you are ready to receive it. The Golden Light is within you It surrounds you always. You can bring your awareness back to it at any time you choose to. It's totally up to you and your intention. Be sure to mentally ground the energy via the Earth Star at your feet at the end of the meditation. You may also like to read the text of the meditation a few times, then meditate for a while and see what comes up for you. You can also record the meditation and listen to the recording as you meditate. Blessings to you as you explore YOUR own INNER Divine Golden Light and shine it out around you.

Gently become aware of the natural flow of your breath as you relax your body, releasing any tension by breathing into the area and saying to yourself "release....let go"...Feel easy...

We call in the five Golden Light Angels of the Elements of Water, Fire, Air, Earth and Ether. Be with us now. Feel Their Presence around you. Drop down into your heart area. Enter your Heart Chakra - your Divine Inner Heart. See yourself seated in the Inner Sacred Space of YOUR heart. See the golden flame burning there. Enter the flame. Surrender to this inner flame in your own heart.
Feel the love. Feel the peace. Feel the power and strength emanating from this Sacred Space which IS you. Feel the Presence of the five Golden Angels of Light. They are with us now and always. They greet you with great love and respect. "We bring you blessings of great joy. We will

purify all your elements if you wish it. It is YOUR choice. We love you beyond all measure and respect your free will."

Continue the meditation if you wish the five Golden Angels of Healing to purify and rejuvenate your five Elements. The great "Agni" (Divine Fire) is lit within your heart. You feel gentle warmth all through your body. You feel a great new strength as the power of love surges through your body, spirit and soul. The Divine Aqua (water) surges through you, cleansing and purifying your feeling elements, gushing out as a fountain from the top of your head centre and washing you with purifying energies. You feel one with the water, swimming in the Ocean of Bliss. The Divine Golden Air "breathes" in your lungs and cleanses your breath. You feel its subtle powers awaken the power of the Divine Breath within and around you. You hear the Divine music - the Cosmic Harmony of the Spheres, playing in your crown chakra. The sound vibrates throughout your whole being. You see the green/blue/golden rays of Mother Earth caressing and supporting you with her powerful, gentle love. You feel very abundant and totally free.

As you continue to be in the space of your own inner heart cave, you see that golden flame burning softly and constantly. This is the inner flame of your own golden heart. The five Golden Angels of healing say to you; See this golden flame burning very brightly. It increases, until your whole heart glows with the Golden Light. Your heart becomes a Golden Heart - see it now - feel the golden energy enveloping you completely and shining throughout your whole being - beyond you into Mother Earth and all Her creatures - into the whole Universe - to all your loved ones (you may name them here). Feel the forgiveness arising, going to all your so called enemies (you may name them here), who now become your friends (if you so choose). You and all of Creation are blessed by the recognition of YOUR own inner Golden Divine Light. You are ONE reality. Meditate for a while in the great Silence of this Divine Source energy as it enfolds you completely. Feel your five elements being purified and recharged as you connect with this Source energy of the Great Silence."

• *meditate for a while ....*

As you gently return to the awareness of your body in the here and now, bring the knowing you have received consciously to the space between your eyebrows (the third eye) and your higher mind (crown chakra). You may like to contemplate this for a while.

We thank our own Golden Hearts, the Golden Angels of the five Elements, Mother Earth and all of Creation for the purification and rejuvenation we have received today. We seal and protect our hearts, all our chakras and nadis (energy grids) with a cross of golden light in a circle of golden light now. It is done. Feel the protection of the Golden Light all around you bringing you comfort and nurturing. You are a Divine Daughter/Son of the Divine Mother/Father of Creation.

Now bring your awareness back to your natural breath. Ground your energy through your feet into Mother Earth. When you are ready, gently open your eyes. Thank yourself for giving YOU an experience of your own Golden Light. You can return to this experience anytime through your intention to do so or by saying the words "Golden Light Angels be with me now and always". Listen in the Silence for Their messages of healing, guidance and comfort. Be at peace with yourself and everyone. Watch how this attitude impacts on YOUR life and the life of those around you. I invite you to see this as an experiment. Watch out for any new findings you come up with.

I thank you with all my heart for your loving participation in this healing meditation. May you be continually blessed by the Divine Golden Light of your own great heart. So be it and so it is!

You may like to email me your healing experiences with this meditation at phueneke@bigpond.com. I would love to hear from you.

Chapter 4. How the Golden Light Essences were created

After my golden light awakening, I kept asking myself what I could do with this new energy. I needed to "ground" it in some way. As usual my life experience gave me the answers. I was invited to teach herbal medicine firstly at the naturopathic course at the Canberra Technical College and I continued to teach a weekly herbal medicine course at my Palmerston clinic. This included guided meditations on the herb or plant we were studying that week. We continued our practical experience of the herb or plant by making tinctures, infusions, cream, ointments, flower essences, infused oils, poultices and extracts of the herb or plant studied each week. I also continued my clinical healing work which gave me great insight into the power of plants and how they could heal people's physical, emotional and spiritual ailments and propel us ever onwards in awareness and growth of consciousness. I also connected more to spiritual healing through the medium of pranic healing and ayurveda. All the time I was experiencing, and still am experiencing, an increasing awareness of this ever expanding Golden Light within me and around me. It manifests in a greater feeling of joy, light heartedness and bliss coming from seemingly nowhere. My loved ones and family and clients certainly commented on how different I had become and some could "see" the Golden Light energy around me.

In 2005/2006 I was asked to teach herbs and iridology at three seminars for Health Schools Australia and as I contemplated this, I had the inspiration to teach about 12 herbs and iris signs for the 12 signs of the zodiac. I had been using this method in prescribing as taught by my naturopathic herbal teacher, Dorothy Hall in 1991-93. I combined this with the ayurvedic method of "Panchakarma" which involves a process of getting into the positive energy or your constitutional type by firstly pacifying the Vata dosha or nervous system. So as I meditated and contemplated this, 12 herbs were made known to me which corresponded to the person types of the 12 signs of the zodiac. It then came to me that the zodiac I needed to use was the Vedic zodiac which is slightly different in time to the Western zodiac commonly used. This made sense to me as I was working with the Ayurvedic system (see Appendix B for a simple explanation of this Ayurvedic system). I taught these 12 nervine herbs, their corresponding Vedic sun sign attributes, healing properties and iris signs at the seminar. It was very well received.

I was then asked to teach another seminar a few months later to the same group of students and I came up with 12 alterative or blood cleansing herbs for the 12 Vedic sun signs and their iris signs. I then realised that before detoxifying with these blood cleansing herbs it would be important to apply the Ayurvedic principal of increasing the Agni, or digestive fire, to burn away the toxins. This stops them flooding the body and making the patient feel more unwell. The herb Ginger is commonly used in Ayurvedic Panchakarma releasing for this purpose. After increasing the digestive fire, it is important to soften and loosen the toxins at the cellular level, so that they can be released more easily. Special herbs in butter ghee are used for this purpose but somehow I couldn't see us westerners using this method, as it is fairly unpalatable. So I thought of the herb Marshmallow, which is used in western herbal medicine to draw out toxins from the cells, ease inflammation and increase adrenal energy, which gives us "fightback" when trying to recover our health. So this is the method I tried with my patients, with good results.

After detoxifying the tissues, the next step in the Ayurvedic Panchakarma treatment is to tone and rejuvenate the tissues and strengthen the once disturbed "dosha, so bringing the person into the positive energy of their constitutional type and Vedic sun sign. As I meditated and contemplated this, I was made aware of 12 herbs which could be used for this purpose. As I taught them to this group of students, I was getting lots of positive feedback using this method of Panchakarma adapted to western cultural healing needs. About 200 clinical patients also reported that they felt more positive and resilient after the treatment. This enabled them to feel more balanced and led to a greater sense of well being and better health. Many had major breakthroughs in their relationships and work life after their personal Panchakarma treatment.

In 2006, I received the Tibetan Blue Medicine Buddha initiation from the Gyuto monks in Australia. I was opened to a greater knowing in my healing work, which gave me increased confidence. Early in 2007, I had the awareness that I could infuse my herbal tinctures and essences with the Golden Light of Healing, through invoking the Golden Angels of Healing of the five elements, who had revealed themselves to me. I had the "knowing" that the 36 herbs of the 12 Vedic sun signs would be a great medium for this purpose and the 36 Golden Light Plant Healing Essences were born. I received the "knowing" of how to make the herbal essences. I grew some of the more unusual plants, such as the Damask Rose, Mugwort, Skullcap, Gardenia, Marshmallow, Peony and many others in my own garden here in Canberra. I also realised that the essences vibrated to the number five for emotional healing and to the fifth Dimension of the Christos Sun energy of the Golden Light and the Golden Angels of Healing. I realised that the essences could clear away lots of emotional karmic issues, very gently and powerfully, bringing us more and more into the reality of our own Golden Divine Light. This was a real breakthrough for me. It gave me the answer I was looking for to the question of "How do I ground the Golden Light Energy into the third dimension of the Earth plane in the here and now?" I could ground the Golden Light energy through the plant kingdom which I had grown to love so much, and had been exploring and using for healing for many years. The five Golden Angels of the purified elements were very willing to assist me in this process. I sensed their Presence all around me constantly. I felt so uplifted.

I continued to make these 36 Golden Light Essences in my clinic from the plant tinctures and flower essences. (See the list of essences at the beginning of this book). I then started to use them, on myself, then my willing family, then my patients. We all reported great results, the most noticeable being the sudden feeling of positive energy and thoughts which arise quite spontaneously when we reconnect with this Golden Light. Difficulties are still there at times, but they dissolve easily, as new awareness arises from within the heart area about how to "solve" this "problem" for the best of everyone concerned. Magic happened! A feeling of "lightness" and "brightness" came over us. We started to "radiate" this Golden Light outwards, all around us. We attracted real "goodness" to ourselves. We felt reconnected to the "Divine" within ourselves. Anything that stood in the way of this positive energy came up for releasing. We found it easy to do so, as we were so supported and loved, bathed in this radiance. Difficult emotional issues just melted into this Golden Light, were absorbed by it, transmuted by it, into love, positivity and new energy. The answers we were seeking just "popped" into our heads, or we would meet someone who would tell us the very thing we wanted to know at that time. W could recognise this and had the energy to act upon it. Our outer life situation changed for the better, our relationships with our loved ones and family improved, we felt more protected, as any negativity was "repelled" by the Golden Light radiating from within us and around us. We started to feel more synchronised with the flow of life, attracting situations and people to us who were naturally helpful. At the same time we were also more willing to be helpful to others. Fear dissolved into love.

In 2009, I taught the 36 (+ 2 of Ginger and Marshmallow) Golden Light Essences from my Golden Light Healing Clinic each week to a group of students for the whole year. We explored making them, discovering their healing powers and meditating on them. Out of this work came the healing information about them which you can discover in the following chapters. You can read about people's healing experiences with the Golden Light Essences and the Golden Angles of Healing. Included are some frequently asked questions (FAQ'S). Enjoy your journey of discovery!

Chapter 5. Healing Experiences with the Golden Light Essences and Meditations

Each of these herb/flower essences was given to patients in my herbal and healing clinic over the past from 1993- 2007. I have also conducted herbal and healing classes each week at my clinic during that time. Each week we examined a herb/plant in detail, made a healing tonic, cream, poultice etc. from the plant and had a direct healing experience of the plant through a guided meditation. Many beautiful healing experiences took place. I am including some of them here.

Please note that everyone quoted here has given me their permission to include their experiences here.

GUIDED MEDITATION ON SKULLCAP:

"During the skullcap meditation, I merged with the skullcap plant. My crossed legs were the leaves, my body was the flower stem, my spine and head became their 'caps'. During the week after this experience, I had rushes of warmth flowing down my right legs (physical side) and into my foot, warming and soothing the spine meridian points. I have an old spinal injury and this felt as if it was sending healing energy to my spine, via the reflexology points in my foot. My spine feels much better." Also *"During the Lotus guided meditation, I was handed an astonishingly beautiful diamond by the goddess Lakshmi. I felt it was a symbol to remind me of my inner jewel – my divinity."*
Student and patient Belinda Canberra

"Pati, thank you for transforming my life and relationships through your intuitive advice and finely tuned herbal expertise. Much love & laughter".
Judy /Canberra

MORE TESTIMONIALS

Iris Golden Light Essence.
"Thank you for allowing me to experience these beautiful essences of yours. I have been applying 3 drops on my wrists and 2 drops under my tongue. When I apply the drops I find myself immediately uplifted into a buoyant and joyous mood with a sense that all things are possible. For a short time afterwards I feel cocooned in the soft loving energy of the golden light helping me feel expanded and connected to the whole. I feel at one with the greater essence of life cocooned in bliss knowing all things are possible. During this time of heightened awareness it is easy to be positive and enthusiastic about life and to know deep within my core that what I dream about is possible and can be realised without a doubt."
Anne, Canberra, June, 2010.

*"I feel such joy and so buoyant after taking the **Hypericum Golden Light Essence.** My mind has calmed down. They have made a huge difference in my life. I have hope again after years of struggle. I can see the light at the end of the tunnel."*
Nils, 2009.

I have been conducting regular **seminars** on attuning and connecting people to the Golden Light and this is was one student said.

"It was such an honour and a privilege to work with Pati and the Golden Light Essences. The day was filled with joy, light and laughter as we worked with the Plant Kingdom and the Golden Angels of healing. The day unfolded like a gentle breeze and we left feeling relaxed, invigorated and very light – golden actually. Thank you Pati, these essences are nothing short of extra-ordinary – simply magical! I am looking forward

to using these 36 boxed stock essences with my clients to assist with emotional release and healing.
Irene (Artist and Kahuna massage therapist), Canberra, 2009.

We also had a great time during the year of 2009 with our weekly study of each of the **36 Golden Light Essences and Meditations.** The students attending the weekly sessions at the Golden Light Healing Clinic contributed greatly to the knowledge of the healing properties of the essences as we discussed, made, used and meditated on them. They were also able to heal and shift a lot of physical and emotional issues and come into their Golden Light energy more and more. Here is what one student who attended all the weekly sessions that year said:

"Pati's Golden Light work with me over the preceding year has left me with much to celebrate in joy. She has given me great hope which no other healing modality could give me. There is much to be said regarding the buoyancy you feel with the Golden Light- the frequency is so enlivening. I wish you all the opportunity to engage with the special nature of the Golden Light and as you find yourself, may you come out and shine with us. Love from the Golden Light Beings and Michelle."
(July, 2010)

The five Panchakarma Golden Light Essence program has been given to many people since 2007. During this program, clients take the five Golden Light Essences for their Vedic sun sign as outlined in Chapter 6. Each essence is taken one at a time, for about two weeks, according to the Ayurvedic guidelines for Panchakarma which include pacifying Vata (the nervous system), increasing Agni (the digestive fire), softening toxins in the cells, cleansing the blood by releasing toxins, and rejuvenating all the tissues.

Here is what some clients said about their experiences with this program and the Golden Light Plant Healing Essences:

The Golden Light essences helped me to give up smoking and alcohol for good after many failed attempts...
"When I met you Pati, I knew that you would be a big part of my life, but had no idea how or how big the journey of awareness would be. When I first started to take the golden light essence, I did not believe much in the power of them. I kept going to you because something inside of me was telling me to and the connection I had with you was a strong one that I did not understand at that time. I continued with *my 5 Panchakarma essence program* for my **Vedic sun sign of Vrishaba/Beauty**. These golden light essences and the pranic spiritual healing you gave me have helped me in many ways I could never have imagined. When I started, I had no idea of the amount of healing I had to do and still have to do. Through your essences and help I have started to release some of the heavy emotions that were weighing me down, such as fear, hurt, anger, shock, guilt, low self worth, lack of trust. I had no idea at the time just how much they were weighing me down. I realised that every "bad" thing that had happened in my life was started by the ego wanting to relive these emotions every day, like a tape playing over and over again. Every time you helped me release more of these emotions, a big weight was lifted from me and I felt more loved and at peace with myself. I also wondered why I had been holding on to this weight for so long.

The Golden Light essences have helped me to quit smoking. Though I had tried to quit so many times before, I had not been successful. I would look at people standing outside and wish I was with them smoking as well. It was always such a struggle and constant battle and I would give in and start smoking again. When you told me, Pati, that you could help me quit with the essences, I had little faith because I had tried so many things. I think I had quit trying to quit smoking. But I had nothing to lose and the essences had helped me with so much already, so I gave it a try. After just a little while I just did not crave for it. I started thinking how 'gross" they are and how much I smelt. I eventually quit 'cold turkey' with the help of the essences, especially the **Plantain Golden Light essence.** I was surprised how easy it was and how I did not want them. I even started to look at people who did smoke and thought:"I'm *so glad I am not trapped anymore." I think that smoking is a thing that we do to keep the bad feelings that the little ego keeps playing over and over again, away from us. When the* **Golden Light Essences** *helped me release some of the bad feelings, it made it easy for me because the feelings were not there anymore. They had been replaced by loving, positive thoughts and feelings.*

I was also able to release the addiction and attachment to alcohol. I did not even know that I had released the attachment until I was thinking about the emotions around it all. I realised that these were the same emotions that I had released while taking my Golden Light essences. The more I release and let go, the more I can hear my own inner self. I now believe in the power of the golden light essences in a big way. Thank you, Pati. I can never thank you enough for the work you have done. I know you will help a lot of lost people, just like I was when I came to see you. I feel I can now see for the first time. The journey has been amazing and I look forward to continuing along the spiritual path with you. Thank you.
Emma, August, 2010.

The Golden Light Essences have improved many aspects of my life in a very practical way…
"The Golden Light essences have been like opening the curtain on a clean window to my soul. I am amazed at how quickly they have affected all aspects of my life. I came to Pati's **Golden Light Healing Clinic** *with a willingness to improve my health, in particular, to remove the anxiety that had controlled my life for at least ten years. I had limited knowledge about Ayurvedic medicine but was intrigued about its workings.*

Within two weeks into my Panchakarma program, I noticed an inner peace that I had never experienced. It was quite overwhelming. Instead of feeling distressed when my children were in fits of tears or tantrums, I was able to maintain a calm and composed state in order to deal with the situation. I no longer feel that my children's behaviour is out of spite; I see what they need and have the clear vision to attend to their needs.

I experience the same enlightenment in my workplace. Being a high school teacher can be stressful, especially when dealing with confrontations with students. I recently intervened in a situation where a student was behaving aggressively towards another teacher. Without thinking, I asked my colleague, who was quite distressed, to leave so that I could speak with the student. (I have never taken charge before!). Despite the student continuing to be aggressive and the other teacher also being defensive, I was surprisingly unaffected by their hostility. I was able to walk away from the situation and not be plagued by the negative vibes. My aura stayed intact. I attribute this new-found calmness to the healing power of the golden light essences.

*By using the **Golden Light Essences**, I now have a tool to help me maintain an inner peace. I sense when my doshas are out of balance and know the path to improve my energy. I will continue to use the golden light essences to help me be a better person, mother and teacher. It has been a wonderful experience.*

Anna, mother of 2, from Dunlop, A.C.T. Australia, August, 2010.

HEALING EXPERIENCES WITH THE 5 GOLDEN ANGELS OF HEALING OF THE ELEMENTS

Recently, I have been connecting with many Light workers and healers online and sending out messages of healing from the Golden Light Angels. Some spontaneous healings have been happening as a result and they moved me very deeply, giving me personally great encouragement to continue my writing and healing work.

In response to a **Face book** entry by **Wild Women,** I replied: "Yes, we are all Golden Divine Light Beings. Keep shining. I am. Can you feel the Golden Light Healing Blessings I am sending you? Here they are right now. Catch them. Golden Light Healing Blessings to all from Pati Solva Hueneke.

I received an answer from **Wild Woman:***"Every day the layers are being removed for me, one by one, and I get closer to this understanding,* *this knowledge of what you have expressed here: Golden Divine Light Beings. Only this morning I have woken to exactly this Golden Light Healing Blessings, repairing a hol(e)y aura and feeling the brightness of my chakra energy system go up in wattage. It is an amazing feeling! Thank you for your message Pati Solva and blessed be.*

Later I received a personal email from the author of the Wild Woman site to explain her message further: *Dear Pati, in relation to our thread earlier, I send this to you and you will see the relevance and why I was so grateful for your words and blessings yesterday. It is in relation to a dream I had this morning when I realised that I had never actually done any healing over a five year relationship that ended five years ago. It was like an OMG moment and I thought some healing needs to be done here.*

So I went into my "boardroom", where I consult with my higher self and it seems that in every chakra the relationship with him had had a really diabolical effect. I had holes in all my chakras and as I lay on my surgery table, we went through the chakras, looking at why they were so damaged. There was lots of light work going on and I called in the healing. It felt really amazing. Imagine it has taken five years to come up and now it has also caused me to realise there is another situation of betrayal that has caused me damage to my aura and chakras and also needs healing. Here is some of my guide's response...
*"Blessings dear one, you are graced with the knowledge of knowing and the power to act accordingly. It is a time of great healing and you are gifted with inner vision to see the damage to your energetic body and the misalignment of your soul purpose. Nothing is ever done without full knowledge of your Self and you chose this path so that you could return in right timing, with full awareness of the power that would be brought into the present with this awakening. So it is time to use this awakened energy which is pure in intention and honed with the power of right action to create a path which is waiting for your footsteps. With compassion for yourself, you can similarly invest that compassion in the many others whose energy you will touch. And it is with this expanded heart space that you will create a **golden awakening** for those who need your direction and foresight that will allow them to glimpse themselves*

through the path that you have walked. **Showers of golden light** *align themselves in your energy field and the brilliance that you emanate is the badge of honour that you wear. We wish to say well done dear one. You found the way back to your heart and you willingly let go of outmoded belief systems so that you could love yourself again. Be gentle with yourself at this time for you are a fragile flower finding its petals basking in the morning light.* **But in the full force of the sun you are a radiant sunflower and the solar energy you are capable of emitting beams a path of intention that paves a path for yourself and others.** *Blessings this day. You are much loved."*

Pati, I am sure you will understand now the relevance of your words and how important it is to follow our intuition. When we feel we should write something - we really should. We never know who we are blessing.
From Wild Woman, August, 2010.

Another client/student wrote:*"Dear Pati, Thank you for all that you have done to help me on my journey. The Golden Light Essences and the Golden Angels of Healing helped turn my life around. I went from someone who was afraid of my own shadow, who was stuck in old patterns, lacked confidence, depressed, a nervous wreck and who suffered panic attacks to someone who exudes confidence, is relaxed and has faith and trust in what is happening. I am also unfazed when teaching yoga to large groups that are new to yoga as well as to those that are more advanced.*

The Golden Light Essences instantly make me feel lighter and relieved – as if a huge weight is lifted off my shoulders. I feel more hopeful and optimistic in whatever situation I am in and easily let go of things that no longer serve me. I also feel more relaxed knowing the Golden Angels of Healing are with me whenever I need them. I often ask them to help me get through a situation, especially if I feel heavy or burdened in some way and they are always on hand to help. I also call on them when doing healings for others and I am always pleasantly surprised with the outcome that happens when the Golden Angels of Healing help out. With love and gratitude."
Sharon, Canberra, August, 2010

FREQUENTLY ASKED QUESTIONS

Q. What is the Golden Light?

A. The Golden Light is an expression of the energy of the life force contained in all of creation. Without this life force we would not be here. It is the energy than enlivens and animates us and it is present in everyone and in everything. It is also our personal connection to the Divine within us and all that this entails. We are always connected to this Golden Light in some way, but as we become more conscious of it, it permeates our thoughts and lives more and more to reveal the beauty of who we really are - Humans made in the Image of the Divine who carry the Divine spark within us. We can let this divine spark grow and grow until it blazes like a fire to purify us and all the physical elements within us like a Divine Alchemy of transformation.

Q. I have the fear that when I do finally have the experience of merging with the Golden Light of the Divine or God, I will lose my individual identity?

A. No, definitely not. You will actually experience more fully the reality of who you really are. The positive aspects of your personality will shine forth more and more and you will live in great bliss and freedom and truth. Life will flow more easily and solutions to so-called 'problems' will present themselves easily and quickly.

Q. Who are the five Golden Light Angels?

A. The five Golden Light Angels are the energies of the Divine within the five elements, water, fire, air, earth and ether. Invoking their powers helps to purify these elements within ourselves and all of creation as the Golden Divine Essence is infused into the material plane of life. These Divine Golden Angels are stepped down from the fifth dimension of reality into our own third dimension to help us live more and more from our own inner divinity. A Divine Alchemy of transformation begins with this purification process. Our world and consciousness of who we really are, are forever changed as we let go and let go more and more of the thoughts, emotions and feelings that keep us trapped in the awareness of the little ego and all the tricks it plays. This Divine Golden energy lives in us all in the centre of the heart chakra and forms the outermost golden layer of our aura. All our subtle bodies are connected to this Golden Light. We can access it as we go deeply into the Great Silence in meditation, or as we choose to remember it in our everyday lives. Doing this brings us into our ultra positive Sun energy and lets life flow more freely and abundantly.

Q. How do the Golden Light Angels help to resolve Karma?

A. The Golden Light Angels are also the five Angels of Karma. They advise us to recognise where we may be reliving old patterns from the past and ask us to release the negative emotions around the issues. The Golden Light Plant Healing essences can be used for this purpose. As we increasingly surrender to the love in our own hearts, these issues are "forgotten" on a cellular level and dissolve. When we live more and more from this Golden Divine Light, we cease to create negative Karma in our lives and ease our own suffering and the suffering of others. You can also do the Panchakarma program with the Golden Light Essences for your Vedic sun sign type (see chapter 6).

Q. I suffer from depression. Can the Golden Light Essences help me?

A. You can take the 5 Golden Light Essence Rescue Remedy (5 Essences of Yarrow, Mugwort, Lotus, Red Clover and Hypericum) as needed. You can do the guided meditation on the Golden Light as often as possible to bring you into more positive energy. You can also look at the table on the Golden Light essences and use your intuition to let the essence which most resonate with you at this time "come out at you". You can order these essences at www.goldenlightessences.com and take them as directed. These essences will bring you into more positive thoughts and feelings as the reasons for your depression start to be resolved. You can also email me for a distance Golden Light essences card reading at phueneke@

bigpond.com to shed some light on the spiritual, emotional and physical issues surrounding your "depression". The essences will not interfere with any medications you may be on. If you have any suicidal thoughts, be sure to seek medical help as soon as possible. Phone Lifeline or a similar helpline in your country.

Q. Can the Golden Light Essences help me to lose weight and maintain a healthy body weight?

A. Yes, the Golden Light Essences will help you to resolve many emotional and spiritual karmic issues which may be associated with maintaining a healthy weight for you personally. As you let go more of these negative thoughts and feelings you may have about your body image, it will become easier to make more positive choices about your eating and drinking and exercise patterns. You will also feel more love and respect for yourself as you move more and more into your own awareness of the Golden Divine Light within you and it is freed to express itself in your life. You can use the Golden Light Essence Divinatory Card Deck to help you "divine" some of your healing issues or you can use your pendulum to "divine" the Golden Light Essences which may assist you at this time. You may also email me for a personal consultation either face to face or online.

Q. Are the Golden Light Essences safe to take?

A. Yes, the Golden Light Essences are very safe and gentle yet powerful in their healing. The Golden Light of Divinity always supports you with great love and compassion and assists you to let go of negativity and move into the positivity of you own inner Sun energy. There may be some temporary healing crises in the form of releases and new awareness which may need to be resolved but the support and energy for healing these are always present with the support of the plants, the Golden Light and the Golden Angels of Healing. You will feel supported and loved in this healing process

Q. Why should I have the awareness of the Golden Light? What would it do for me?

A. The awareness of the Golden Light is always with you on some level of your inner knowing. It is your natural state as a human being created in the image of your Creator. Recognition of this will enhance your life in every possible way. Any fear, anxiety, feeling of lack, grief, sadness, anger, pain etc. will "dissolve" or melt way in the great fire of this golden light. You will feel "lighter", more at ease with yourself and others, and find it easier to "let go" or release any emotions, feelings, life situations and relationships which are not bringing you joy, peace and love. The Golden Light is your support in your life path here on earth. It gives you renewed energy for living, attracting more positive life experiences to you and easing "suffering" as you gain deeper insight into true life purpose in this lifetime. You may get the "knowing" that your life here in matter on the earth plane is to serve the growth of your Spirit and the expansion of your Soul. You may feel more connected with all of life and not so separate from everything and everyone. Feelings of loneliness subside. I could go on an on but I think you get my "drift".

Chapter 6. The 36 (+2) Golden Light Essences and their healing qualities, properties and symptom pictures

You can use the following description of the healing properties of the plants of the Golden Light Essences to guide you in your therapeutic use of them. I have included a person picture of the Vedic sun sign (see the table at the end of this chapter to determine your Vedic sun sign according to your birth date) for each of the essences, although each essence may also be taken by any Vedic sun sign type if indicated, as we are all moving into the wholeness of the Zodiac or into the Oneness of all of creation. As we heal the issues that may come up for us during our life experience here on earth, we move more and more into this Oneness or Wholeness of Being. Our connection to our own inner Golden Light becomes stronger and stronger. You can gauge this connection changing as the outer circumstances of your life also change and as you feel and see yourself moving along your path in life more freely rather than feeling "stuck" in a groove.

This information can help you in the choice of essence you may like to take at any time and you can also "divine" your essence with your pendulum or the divinatory card deck which goes with the essences. You may also just "feel" on an intuitive level that a particular essence may help you move through a problem you may have at the moment. Remember to consult a health or medical professional for any medical problems you may have. These essences are intended to compliment your health and wellbeing care and move you forward on your life's journey, into a greater awareness and experience of the Golden Light.

They can bring you into a more positive frame of mind and dissolve negative thoughts and work well with affirmations.

Please see **Appendix A** at the end of the book for a list of common ailments and the best Golden Light Essence/s to use for your healing. At the end of these essence descriptions you can also read about how to use them for your personal 10 week Panchakarma or purification treatment. All the essences are available from my website and online shop at www.goldenlightessences.com
Happy Golden Light Essence Healing!

1. ALFALFA GOLDEN LIGHT ESSENCE

(Medicago sativa)
Major nervine to pacify *Vata*.
Plant Family: Papilonaceae/Leguminosae
Common Names: Lucerne, Purple medick.
Parts Used: leaves, flowers, stem as tincture, tea.

Keywords: *I haven't got time now!*

<u>Alfalfa Golden Light Essence</u> is a great antioxidant and tonic to the whole nervous system. It helps to heal heart disease and stroke and some cancers by removing carcinogens in the colon. The chlorophyll it contains brings freshness to the breath and cleanses lymph.

"I haven't got time now" - this is the *Alfalfa person* on the go. Too much to do and too little time! They appreciate beauty and like to have TIME to complete tasks. They like to work in their own time. They are not fast. They are slow and deliberate in their actions. When the heat is on they can keep a cool head but often suffer afterwards. They are sensitive and intuitive folk. They "sniff" out the atmosphere and vibes around them before they act. They need to wait "for the right time". If they are hurried by time deadlines, they may get out of balance which can lead to a "pickling" or an acid, irritating condition in their nervous systems. If pushed too far they can "vent their spleen", putting stress on the lymphatic system. Their digestive systems can get acidic too. Proteins may be difficult to digest. Skin sensitivity may cause bad reaction to insect bites and stings. Mucous membranes may overreact to irritants causing inflammation, itchiness, swelling and chronic catarrh of the nose and throat.

<u>Alfalfa Golden Light Essence</u> can pacify aggravated nervous systems and bring them back into balance. The nutritive substances in Alfalfa assist this function. The positive *Alfalfa* loves beauty and makes time their servant, not their master.

2. BURDOCK GOLDEN LIGHT ESSENCE

(Arctium lappa)
Major alterative to detoxify tissues.
Plant Family: Compositae/Asteraceae
Common Names: Cocklebur, Personata,
Parts Used: leaf, root seeds.

Keywords: *I unmask the real Self.*

The person needing <u>Burdock Golden Light Essence</u> often masks their true feelings and symptoms. They can suffer from kidney pain, gout, sciatica; pain in the ankles, feet and hips and thighs. Congestion and inflammation in the pelvic organs is worse for standing for long periods. Skin symptoms of acne, boils, abscesses, swelling and redness are common. There can be a mask-like redness over the cheeks and nose, sore throats. Uterine prolapse (burdock is the uterine magnet), thrush and dropsy (water retention) can all be treated with <u>Burdock Golden Light Essence</u> in 5 drop doses, twice daily for about 3 weeks. They can have feet pain, bunions, hammer toes and contraction of tendons; rheumatic and arthritic pains, gout and sciatica.

The hips and thighs rule the *Dhanus* vedic sun sign person who, like the horse or centaur, often has a weakness in this area. They can have congestion and inflammation here which can interfere with the blood flow and nerve supply to the pelvic organs, kidneys, legs and feet, causing red hot pain, boils and abscesses. Their passionate, fire-sign nature can need a little cooling off sometimes as they find out that not everyone shares their unbridled enthusiasm for life in quite the same way as they do. They can suffer from the unmasking of their feelings and emotions to show the delusion of dualism or they may be totally mistaken about an issue, which can give them a "red face" of embarrassment. Burdock with its high content of silicon (the Dhanus cell salt) can help to cleanse and strengthen the tissues and nerves, giving more "horsy" stamina and endurance to weather the storms and challenges of life. <u>Burdock Golden Light Essence</u> helps them to see the truth.

3. CHAMOMILE GOLDEN LIGHT ESSENCE

(Matricaria recutita)
Major nervine to pacify *Vata*.
Plant Family: Compositae/Asteracea.
Common Names: Maythen, Chamaimelon, Ground Apple, Manzanilla (Spanish), Heermanchen (German).
Parts Used: flowers; whole plant.

Keywords: *I calm any battle of wills.*

Chamomile Golden Light Essence 5 drops, twice daily may be used for headaches, indigestion, colic, bad effects of anger and strong emotions, eye inflammations, jaundice, digestive and nervous problems of children, painful periods and absence of periods, mastitis, to ease childbirth, for asthma and allergic reactions . At dinner time the *Chamomile* is so exhausted from retelling the dramatic events of the day (which were really just ordinary), that they can't eat at all. "I've got such a stomach ache." At night they toss and turn. "I can't sleep at all. My mind and body are totally hyperactive. Give me some Chamomile". "Oh, what a relief"! Calm descends! "Oh! How soothing, how comforting! I think I'll go to sleep now". Peace and harmony at last!

Kataka vedic sun signs are sensitive, water sign folk who can't bear pain. "I can't bear myself. I can't bear you. I can't bear anything. Everything is simply intolerable. Go away and leave me alone. No, come back and listen to me."This is the *Kataka Chamomile* when they are having adrenal burnout and are out of harmony with themselves and others. You just can't do anything to please them. Life becomes a battle of wills between parent and child, child and child; a battle of wills within themselves. "Will I do this? Will I do that? What should I do? I don't know what to do? It is all too painful! I think I'll just slump in this chair."

4. COMFREY GOLDEN LIGHT ESSENCE

(Symphytum officinalis)
Major tonic to rejuvenate tissues
Plant Family: Boraginaceae
Common Names: Knitbone, Common Comfrey, Bruisewort,
Slippery Root, Boneset, Consolida, Consound.
Parts Used: flowers.

Keywords: *I unite. I make whole.*

Comfrey Golden Light Essence is a tonic to the spleen, bones, skin and nerves. The person needing comfrey can often feel the strain of the earthly journey very acutely. They love to really get into life, often pushing them to the limit of human endurance. This tendency can put real strain on nerves, bones, skin and connective tissue. They often have trouble with joints too. Many have had knee problems by the time they reach adulthood. The Saturnian ruled *Makara* can get great comfort and healing from Comfrey Golden Light Essence which is also a plant of Saturn and cooling in its quality. This cooling quality helps to soothe inflammation which often comes after physical injuries.

The long climb of the mountain goat up the summit of achievement in life requires great perseverance and endurance. Along the way they often have accidents and injuries requiring periods of rest and recuperation. They need a tonic to give them new energy and strength for life's journey and for learning the hard life lessons that stern Saturn often brings to us. Comfrey Golden Light Essence can also help to bring the new understanding required to learn these hard Saturnian lessons.

5. DAMASK ROSE GOLDEN LIGHT ESSENCE

(Rosa damascene)
Major tonic to rejuvenate tissues.
Plant Family: Rosaceae.
Common Names: Queen of flowers,
Parts Used: flowers and leaves.

Keywords: *Opening the Heart chakra / Divine Love.*

Damask Rose Golden Light Essence is an excellent remedy to lift the heart energy and ease depression. It is also a tonic to the adrenals and kidney chi, easing anxiety and emotional shocks. It can be used in 5 drop doses, twice daily over a 3 week period to ease digestive problems, dry skin, hormonal problems, heart palpitations, lung and bronchial infections, hay fever and on an emotional level to increase love energies and to open the heart and ease tension and pain. Rose oil eases muscular tension and is excellent oil for massage to bring peace and relaxation. Rose syrup is used for sore throats and bronchitis, soothing inflamed mucous membranes. Infusions of rose petals are a great tonic to the capillaries.

Tulas can have a constitutional weakness in the paired organs of the kidneys, adrenals, lungs and thyroid and Damask Rose Golden Light Essence can act as a rejuvenating tonic to balance the energies in these organs and to lift the heart energy, making it easier for them to make decisions and to feel less anxiety and agony about the decisions once made. Ruled by Venus, the planet of love and beauty, *Tulas* can derive great benefit from the energy of the damask rose, to bring their heartfelt desires into action. It can also calm any nervous tension they may feel about love relationships and intimacy with others. It helps to cool any heated emotions bringing balance and harmony into their lives. Damask rose brings the energy of gentleness and divine love, rejuvenating the body, mind, heart and soul at a cellular level, renewing the etheric and emotional bodies. The *Tula* sun can shine out balanced love and harmony once more.

6. ELDERFLOWERS GOLDEN LIGHT ESSENCE

(Sambucus nigra)
Major alterative to detoxify tissues.
Plant Family: Caprifoliaceae.
Common Names: Common elder, Pipe tree, Hollunder
Parts Used: flowers, berries, bark, and root.

Keywords: *Fairy magic, magic wands; death,*
rebirth and renewal - "the complete medical chest".
Opens the "tubes" of the body – blood vessels, lungs, skin, kidneys.

<u>Elderflower Golden Light Essence</u> gives us a renewed faith and self confidence in our own strength for recovery. The "elder' mother protects and supports us in this death of the old and rebirth of new energy. We are totally nurtured by this strong "Divine Mother Magic".

Makara people are the builders of the zodiac and can have weaknesses in the bones, skin and teeth as well as the mucous membranes of the body. They can be hypersensitive to their environment which may lead to allergies of all kinds, fevers associated with upper respiratory infections in childhood, with nightmares and disturbed dreams. The high fevers can lead to an overheated and congested condition of the blood and possible convulsions. They need the opening, cleansing and supportive action of the elderflower "mother" to strengthen the matrix of the bones, teeth and skin and to absorb calcium phosphate better through the gastro-intestinal tract (mucosa).

Makara vedic sun signs need to build inner strength and self esteem and calming of their fears and anxieties. They need to feel protection from harm or evil and of over domination by others. They feel secure as their belief in the death/rebirth cycle of life is confirmed by the awareness of their innate powers of recovery and renewal of energy. Now they can build anew, opened to the beauty aspect of Venus, *Holda*, the Divine Mother and protector.

7. FENUGREEK GOLDEN LIGHT ESSENCE

(Trigonella foenum-graecum)
Major nervine to pacify *Vata*.
Plant Family: Leguminosae (peas).
Common Names: Bird's Foot, Hay Seed, Methi (Sanskrit).
Parts Used: seeds and aerial parts.

Keywords: *I bring nutrition to cells.*

Fenugreek Golden Light Essence may be taken in 5 drop doses, twice daily for 3 weeks to improve nerve function to the liver, lungs, digestive system, urinary and reproductive systems and brings improved nutrition to all cells. *Fenugreek* people love the good things of life – rich food, good wines, beautiful clothes, homes, cars, artworks etc. Very often they work very hard and for long hours to earn the money to buy these things of beauty. They show great loyalty to their employers and to their families and loved ones, often trying to provide for them in every way they possibly can. In the process, they may get very sedentary, stressed and lack the time for exercise. Getting into nature or regular exercise is a great boost for them, but they often lack the nervous energy to get started.

Fenugreek Golden Light Essence can help them get out of the workplace and into the leisure/exercise space. This gets their lymphatic systems pumping and the toxins in the nervous system clearing out, bringing better muscle tone and reshaping that podgy tummy. Blood pressure is lowered, liver function improved and any excess fluid washed away. They start to sweat more from the exercise and eliminate toxins via the skin, clearing away blemishes and clogging in the pores. Overall, Fenugreek can help to balance work and play for the ambitious (*Makara*) person, making the climb to the top of the mountain a more pleasant, loyal and healthy life experience. They may also discover that what they need most is loyalty to their own inner goals.

8. GARDENIA GOLDEN LIGHT ESSENCE

(Gardenia ssp)
Major tonic to rejuvenate tissues
Plant Family: Rubiaceae.
Common Names: Gardenia Florida.
Parts Used: flowers, fruits, leaves and stems.

GARDENIA

Keywords: *I activate intuition.*
I clear the third eye chakra.

Gardenia Golden Light Essence has a tonic action on the blood, reducing heat and dampness. It quells fire and is used for reducing fevers, inflamed eyes and acute liver conditions such as hepatitis. The fruit is used widely in Chinese medicine for deficient *Liver Blood*, which may have symptoms of period pains and headaches. Gardenia can be used for spiritual emergencies such as heightened emotional states, physical accidents, heat induced bleeding etc. to calm and clear the sixth chakra or third eye, giving a feeling of complete protection and comfort.

Kumba's constitutional weak spots are the shins and ankles and the circulation. Gardenia Golden Light Essence can act as a tonic to these areas in the physical body. *Kumba* people are also very open to physic disturbances due to their great concerns for the welfare of humanity in general. They need to get a balanced perspective in their concern for themselves and for others. Anger, resentment and heat build up in the liver and blood as they cry out, "how unfair". They can take on the wrongs of the world. What a great burden. Often they forget about their own needs in this whole process of caring for the world. They do not "guard" or protect themselves, their families and their close relationships in their great work of healing the injustices and cruelties of the world. They can seem aloof to those they love. Gardenia Golden Light Essence can help *Kumbas* to realise that they are connected to all and that as they change themselves, so that positive change will be reflected around them. In this way they may be able to make a difference of healing one person at a time and feel less stressed in the process. This is the insight they may gain.

9. GENTIAN GOLDEN LIGHT ESSENCE

(Gentiana lutea)
Major alterative to cleanse tissues
Plant Family: Gentianaceae.
Common Names: Enzian, Bitterwort
Parts Used: root and flower.

Keywords: *I dispel doubt. I bring certainty.*

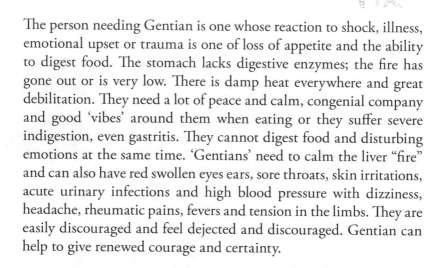

The person needing Gentian is one whose reaction to shock, illness, emotional upset or trauma is one of loss of appetite and the ability to digest food. The stomach lacks digestive enzymes; the fire has gone out or is very low. There is damp heat everywhere and great debilitation. They need a lot of peace and calm, congenial company and good 'vibes' around them when eating or they suffer severe indigestion, even gastritis. They cannot digest food and disturbing emotions at the same time. 'Gentians' need to calm the liver "fire" and can also have red swollen eyes ears, sore throats, skin irritations, acute urinary infections and high blood pressure with dizziness, headache, rheumatic pains, fevers and tension in the limbs. They are easily discouraged and feel dejected and discouraged. Gentian can help to give renewed courage and certainty.

Vedic *Kataka* sun signs can have a constitutional weakness in the stomach and digestive system. The water/fire balance can be disturbed in these sensitive souls by upsetting emotions, environments and people to the point where they feel too debilitated to eat at all. The disturbed digestive system can lead to symptoms of nausea, heartburn, flatulence and pain. On an emotional level, people needing *Gentian* can suffer setbacks easily which lead them to doubt in their own inner healing abilities, leading to depression and lassitude. They can get caught up in a negative spiral of debilitating thoughts and feelings. Gentian Golden Light Essence can 'detoxify' these 'poisons' and bring back a feeling of certainty and faith in 'digesting' life's experiences and seeing the positive in every life situation. They become more optimistic about the future and more able to live in the present moment and to reclaim their own positive personal power. The solar plexus becomes balanced as the water/ fire elements are cleansed, restored and calmed. They become more resilient and better able to cope with life.

10. GOLDEN SEAL GOLDEN LIGHT ESSENCE

(Hydrastis candensis)
Major alterative to detoxify tissues.
Plant Family: Ranunculaceae (Buttercups).
Common Names: Yellow Root, Eye Balm.
Parts Used: root, whole plant, flowers.

Keywords: *I have faith in my own inner Divinity.*

Golden Seal Golden Light Essence tones the mucosa throughout the body, especially in the digestive tract, sinuses, ears, throat etc. It can be taken in 5 drop doses twice daily for 10-14 days for infections with thick, stringy, yellow mucous discharges, for allergies and food sensitivities, skin conditions such as impetigo, ulcers, hay fever, vaginal discharges, obstinate constipation, arthritis, and lack of faith, stubbornness and anger. It has been used with other treatments for some cancers.

The Vedic sun sign of *Vrishaba* rules the throat and thyroid gland. *Vrishaba* people often have heat and sensitivity to emotional and environmental toxins, which can inflame mucous membranes throughout the whole body. After a while, the immune system can be compromised, leading to a hypo/under-functioning of the stomach, liver and gallbladder and musculature, including the heart muscle. The solar plexus is weakened too. *Vrishaba* people tend to be stoic and stubborn about their condition and lack faith in their own healing ability. They often harden themselves to people and the world around them, resulting in a hardening of the blood vessels and joints (arthritis). They may also find it difficult to speak about their inner feelings, causing a blockage at the throat chakra.

Golden Seal Golden Light Essence can restore *Vrishaba's* faith in their innate healing abilities and reconnect them to the source of divine healing within. It can "seal" the leakage of energy at the solar plexus and restore the vitality of the digestive system, cleansing the blood and healing the mucous membranes, bringing beauty and radiance. Golden Seal can act like a detergent throughout the body, cleansing sore throats and tonsils and protecting the immune system from attack both within and without. The *Vrishaba* sun becomes balanced again and they can enjoy life's beauty and pleasures once more.

11. HOPS GOLDEN LIGHT ESSENCE

(Humulus lupulus)
Major nervine to pacify *Vata*.
Plant Family: Articaceae.
Common Names: Hopfen, Wild Hops,
Parts Used: the flowers (strobiles).

Keywords: *I transform Shame into Honour!*

<u>Hops Golden Light Essence</u> is given in 5 drop doses, twice daily to restore adrenal function, ease insomnia, aid digestion and sluggish liver function due to a stressed nervous system. Hops can rebalance the nervous system, reducing anxiety and tension in muscles. Spasms in the digestive system and irritable bowel syndrome are eased. The bitters stimulate the secretion of bile and digestive juices. Emotional tension is also eased with hops and group interaction is improved. Feelings of clumsiness and shame are eased. The intuitive function increases and the sixth chakra is cleansed and opened. There is a greater attuning to God's plan in our lives that causes the nervous system to relax more.

Tulas often find it hard to make decisions as they weigh up and plan for every possibility, which become impossible. Stress and tension result as their nervous system and adrenals become worn out with all this pre-planning. When things go wrong, or don't go according to plan, they can get frustrated and angry, which puts further stress on the liver and digestive system. Imbalance is the result. They find it hard to get to sleep at night as their minds are pre-planning the next day and they wake up exhausted. They have lived their day and all the stresses involved before the day has even started. Then they find that their plans go haywire as circumstances change completely. The result is adrenal overload, liver congestion, frayed nerves and tense, painful muscles. Sometimes making any decisions is just too much hard work so they sit on the fence waiting for things to happen. This makes them impatient and intolerant. Oh what a mess! <u>Hops Golden Light Essence</u> can calm *Tulas'* anxiety about decision making and bring their nervous systems back into balance. They can trust more in their own intuition about their true life plan and go with the divine flow more easily. Balance is restored.

12. HYPERICUM GOLDEN LIGHT ESSENCE

(Hypericum perforatum)
Major nervine to pacify *Vata*.
Plant Family: Hypericaceae.
Common Names: Herb of St.John, Johnswort,
Sol Terrestis, Amber, Flower of Light/fairies.
Parts Used: flowers, whole plant, leaves
(perforations contain essential oils, red in colour, "heart of Jesus oil").

Keywords: *New Age Healing. Nerve regeneration.*

Hypericum is a specific herb for injuries to nerve endings and for hypersensitivity of the five senses via the skin. Hypericum Golden Light Essence may be used in 5 drop doses for injured nerves, (e.g. after surgery), for injuries caused by a sharp instrument or needle, for trigeminal neuralgia, neuritis, neuroses, nervous debility and depression, abdominal pain, spinal pain (especially coccyx), for burns and blisters, sciatica, rheumatism, bed wetting, hysteria, gout, arthritis, coughs and viral/bacterial infections, shingles. It is a wonderful remedy for nerve pain and repairs any trauma to the nervous system after injuries. Hypericum brings light to dispel darkness.

People born under the vedic sun sign of *Dhanus* often have a highly reactive nervous system and can get "spooked" quite easily. They usually hate needles, the dentist or any physical pain. Their skin can be quite sensitive to many substances and may break out in rashes, hives, red blotches which can be very painful. They may be clumsy or un-coordinated at times. Touch is very soothing for their five senses and they love wearing soft fabrics such as silk and cotton. They hate scratchy materials such as wool. They can be speedy people who want to get as much experience of life as they can in the shortest possible time. They can be very impatient. Their nervous systems can get over-stimulated and irritated physically, bringing with it nerve ending pain, inflammation of the skin from stings, bites, viral rashes, shingles, prickly heat, dermatitis etc.

They need the soothing balm of Hypericum Light Essence to soothe and tone their irritated physical nerves.

13. HYSSOP GOLDEN LIGHT ESSENCE

(Hyssopus officinalis)
Major tonic to rejuvenate tissues.
Plant Family: Lamiaceae.
Common Names: Hyssop Herb, Isopo, Ysopo.
Parts Used: leaf and flowers.

Keywords: *I transform Guilt into FORGIVENESS.*

Hyssop Golden Light Essence is an excellent tonic for the lungs and respiratory system, enhancing immunity, decongesting the bronchia, easing and breaking up catarrh, resolving infection, toning mucous membranes and by its expectorant action, easing coughs and colds. It can also be used as a gargle for sore throats and tonsillitis. It eases allergic components of hay-fever or asthma and brings down fevers. Hyssop can act as a nerve tonic for the lungs, relieving anxiety, tension, spasms by its calming action.

On an emotional level the Hyssop Golden Light Essence can be used to purify and cleanse the emotional body, calm the stormy waters and to bring the true understanding of forgiveness for yourself and others. It can lighten any burdens of guilt, especially in family conflicts. As an oil, hyssop can be rubbed into painful joints and bring relief from pain. It can also be used for cold sore (herpes simplex). The essence can be taken in 5 drop doses, twice daily over a period of three weeks. Hyssop also acts as a tonic to the digestive system by its bitter action, assisting the liver and gallbladder. It brings a feeling of peace and forgiveness, releasing guilt and giving true healing to the emotional and physical body. The vedic *Maithuna* sun rules the lungs and nervous system. The air prana, the inflowing and out-flowing breath needs to be in harmony to calm their sensitive nervous systems. Erratic breathing patterns can bring a disturbance in the nerve supply to the lungs, causing asthma, bronchial and lung infections. Hyssop acts as a rejuvenating tonic to these systems. The emotions of guilt are transmuted into forgiveness. The third chakra and the emotional body are cleansed and toned. Tension is relieved and the gold element is better assimilated with <u>Hyssop Golden Light Essence</u>. Calm at last to those jumpy, wheezy *Maithunas.*

14. IRIS GOLDEN LIGHT ESSENCE

(Iris versicolour)
Major alterative to detoxify tissues.
Plant Family: Iridaceae.
Common Names: Blue Flag, Wild, Fleur-de-lis, Flag Lily.
Parts Used: whole plant, root, and flower.

Keywords: *I reconnect you to your rainbow bridge which links heaven and earth.*

People needing Iris present with wild changes of thyroid metabolism causing mood swings from depression to elation, which are totally unpredictable. These are tied to thyroid dysfunction, which swings from under-active to overactive because of an erratic distribution of hormones from the pituitary. They can also have low and high blood sugar levels, due to pancreatic dysfunction and insulin resistance. There can be red, dry skin rashes, a feeling of paralysis in various parts (tight tendons), especially in the legs and respiratory system. In the digestive tract there is nausea and vomiting, weight gain, addictive food habits, a sunburnt, glazed appearance of the skin over the face and neck, and a burning sour feeling in the stomach and mouth. They need renewed *trust* in their own inner divinity.

Emotionally there is a feeling of being low-spirited and easily discouraged – a feeling of being stuck in the mud. There is a feeling of inner emptiness of spirit and separation from the inner source of divine love in the heart. Iris can help to re connect to this inner spiritual source of divine guidance.

People born under the Vedic sun sign of *Maithuna* often need cleansing so that the personal will can be brought into closer alignment with the will of the Divine. A letting go or surrender to the Divine higher self takes place out of an inner conflict leading to a healing crisis. Grace descends as an ability to transcend the earthly "stuck in the mud" experience and ride the rainbow bridge to the world of light. <u>Iris Golden Light Essence</u> can help with this process. New creative insights result. The *Maithuna* sun at the heart and solar plexus is cleansed and purified. Life becomes simple again and harmony descends. The *Maithuna* twins can work together as a united force, inspired by the light of the rainbow. The digestive system feels easy. The heart feels secure and peaceful. The heat in the physical body is balanced with the water element. Problems are not dwelt on but "jumped over". Hormones become balanced. Sensitivities are transformed into resilience and stamina. Blood sugar levels become steady and energy distribution more even. *Maithunas* can shine the light from their inner spirit once more.

15. KELP GOLDEN LIGHT ESSENCE

(Fucus vesiculoṣus)
Major tonic to rejuvenate tissues.
Plant Family: Algae/Fucaceae.
Common Names: Sea-Wrack, Kelp-Ware, Black-Tang, Sea Spirit.
Parts Used: dried mass of root, stem and leaves (Thallus)

Keywords: *Help, I need some Kelp. Communicating with the Source.*

Kelp has been used traditionally to treat a condition of the thyroid called goitre and to disperse tumours and swellings of the glands. It also is an aid to increasing metabolism and has been used in many slimming preparations. A liniment is made from the sea-pod to relieve rheumatic pains. It can also increase digestion and diminish flatulence; it can ease obstinate constipation. Kelp provides many nutrients to the body, especially iodine and helps to dissolve mucous in the respiratory tract.

The Vedic sun sign of *Vrishaba* rules the neck and throat and the organs associated with these areas – the thyroid and glands around the neck. Kelp Golden Light Essence has an affinity with the throat and is a nutritive tonic to the thyroid and glandular system. Its demulcent action can dissolve swellings and tumours and can stimulate the thyroid or balance its action, remove goitres and stimulate metabolism. It helps the weary *Vrishaba* find their way back to the Source energy for deep healing and renewal of spiritual and physical energy. Any harshness is transmuted into the beauty of Venus once more.

The sea and moon energies of kelp lead to deep emotional healing and a renewed commitment to the spiritual path of Self knowledge. This helps the *Vrishaba* person to see life from the perspective of compassion, mercy and forgiveness, opening the way to initiation into the Neptunian mysteries of the deep ocean of life, death and renewal. They can get a glimpse of the eternal beauty of unconditional love from within their own divinity once again.

16. LAVENDER GOLDEN LIGHT ESSENCE

(Lavendula officinalis)
Major tonic to rejuvenate tissues.
Plant Family: Lamiaceae.
Common Names: Elf Leaf, Nard, Nardus, Spike,
Our Lady's Candlestick.
Parts Used: whole plant in flower, flower heads.

Keywords: *I remove karmic blockages to*
stimulate spiritual growth. I clear the Crown chakra.

Lavender eases nervous tension in the neck and shoulders and is a good treatment for migraines and insomnia. It rejuvenates the nervous system and the capillary bed. The essential oil can be diluted in almond oil for a relaxing massage and used on the *herpes simplex* virus (cold sores). Lavender can be used to dispel flatulence, combat putrid bacteria in the intestines, to ease fainting and dizzy spells and to stop nausea and vomiting (travel sickness). It can be used as an ointment to ease the pain of arthritis and rheumatism and as an antiseptic for wounds and insect bites. Hildegard of Bingen says it can bring "pure knowledge and clear understanding". It can ease the symptoms of pre-menstrual tension and so-called "female hysteria".

The Vedic sign of *Kanya* rules the neck and shoulders and the small intestine where the nutrients are absorbed into the bloodstream via the capillary bed. Lavender Golden Light Essence is excellent to support this process. *Kanyas* are often "perfectionists" in all that they do which can in time lead to a depletion of the nervous system and "nervous breakdown". They can work themselves into a state of "hysteria" and "frazzle".

Lavender can soothe tone and rejuvenate their nerves, bringing them the new awareness and understanding that whatever life experiences we have are just perfect in their own way for our highest spiritual and physical good; not just for us personally but for all concerned.

This understanding allows the nervous system to be in a state of tranquillity and the mind to be calm. They can then flow calmly with the process of life instead of wanting to make things happen. In time the depleted nervous system will recover.

17. LEMON BALM GOLDEN LIGHT ESSENCE

(Melissa officinalis)
Major nervine to pacify *Vata*.
Plant Family: Lamiaceae.
Common Names: Bee Balm, Lemon Balsam,
Melissa, Sweet Balm.
Parts Used: Flower, leaves, stems.

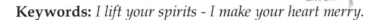

Keywords: *I lift your spirits - I make your heart merry.*

Lemon Balm was used by the ancients as a remedy for melancholy, to "make the heart merry" and to promote a long life. It was called the "elixir of life". It is used to bring down high blood pressure and to ease dizziness in the head (vertigo). It eases indigestion, flatulence, colic, stimulates liver and gallbladder and nervous upsets in the digestive tract. It is a specific for cold sores and heals wounds of insect bites, nose bleeding, temple headaches, and tinnitus and thyroid problems. Lemon Balm is good to use for circulatory problems, stroke prevention, aneurisms and thrombosis. It also helps with urinary problems, eye problems, heart palpitations and baldness. It relieves anxiety and worry. It is a truly soothing and healing balm, gently but powerfully healing the nervous system and calming "moony" emotions and stresses. <u>Lemon Balm Golden Light Essence</u> can be taken in 5 drop doses twice daily for about 25 days to calm and balance the nervous system and relieve some of these conditions.

Meena folk are ruled by the watery moon energies and often feel their emotions very acutely. They pick up on the prevailing emotional energies around them and find it hard to maintain their boundaries. Confusion results as to what feelings and emotions belong to them and to those around them, especially with their loved ones. They worry constantly, suffer fear and anxiety and often find themselves waiting to hear news or a message about the outcome of events. This puts strain on their nervous systems, kidneys (fear), brain, circulatory system (blood pressure) and heart bringing melancholia and lethargy. The nerves near the surface of the skin become sensitive and they suffer allergies and intolerances. How soothing the <u>Lemon Balm Golden Light Essence</u> is for these anxious Meena folk! They can think clearly again as the dizziness and fog lifts from their minds and brains. They can discriminate better between their own emotions and feelings and those of others. Personal boundaries become more defined. Lethargy lifts as their energies return. They can navigate the waters of the emotions more freely and with greater accuracy allowing them to feel true compassion for themselves and others without stress and anxiety.

18. LOTUS GOLDEN LIGHT ESSENCE

(Nelumbo nucifera)
Major tonic to rejuvenate tissues.
Plant family: Nymphaeaceae.
Common Names: Red Lily, Sacred Lotus, Padma(Buddhist).
Parts Used: flowers, plumes, seeds, roots, and leaves.

Keywords: *Jewel of enlightenment, uniting the Chakras.*

Lotus Golden Light Essence can be used to remedy many crown chakra/brain symptoms such as vagueness, indecisiveness, lack of focus, daydreaming (excess of), headaches, emotional disturbances, poor nutrition to the brain clearing negative thought patterns, injuries and inflammation to the brain. It helps us to feel grounded, focused and living in the present moment. Lotus Golden Light Essence can be used in 5 drop doses, twice daily for about 3 weeks as a tonic to the heart and circulatory system. The seeds can be used for insomnia, fertility tonic and lack of appetite. The root can be eaten as a food as a rejuvenating tonic to the digestive system, kidneys (cystitis), and for recovery from illness.

The *Meesha's* sun rules the head and the brain. This raw energy of the mind needs to be grounded and focused and the "fool" energy which propels us forward into new awareness needs light and transmutation. Lotus Golden Light Essence can act as the healing, alchemical "philosopher's stone" in this process. Emotional problems are eased. The crown chakra is energized and all the chakras, meridians, nadis and subtle bodies are temporarily aligned and balanced. Lotus seed aids in the assimilation of all nutrients and regenerates the tissues at a cellular level. The head and brain can recover from any injuries it may have received. Thinking becomes clearer. The "child" of the zodiac can "grow up" into adulthood and maturity and resume its rightful place of leadership in its world. The child-like qualities of innocence and purity are recovered. The positive *Meesha* qualities of the inner child become receptive again to the divinity within the heart, opening the heart to receive the gifts of the divine - the light within the heart - the Jewel within the Lotus of the Heart. Lotus can help link our heart to the heart of the Divine and the heart of the Sun. This is sometimes called the triple 8 energy of infinity (888) and completely restores our heart energy.

19. MARY'S THISTLE GOLDEN LIGHT ESSENCE

(Silybum marianum)
Major tonic to rejuvenate tissues.
Plant Family: Asteraceae.
Common Names: Variegated Thistle, Our Ladies Milk Thistle.
Parts Used: whole plant -roots, leaves, flowers and seeds.

Keywords: *I protect the Liver (ruled by Jupiter).*
I heal melancholia and bring joy.

Pain in liver and spleen, ache in left scapula, varicose veins, congestion of liver, spleen and kidneys, portal vein congestion, alcoholism, hepatitis B, biliousness, gallstone colic, swelling of liver and then cirrhosis, oedema of abdominal area, indigestion, heat and dry skin, ropy veins on arms and legs, haemorrhoids, pelvic congestion, chronic cough and bronchitis, jaundice, fatty liver, pains in joints of the feet, mushroom poisoning, toxins in liver from medications or chemotherapy. Emotional symptoms of anger and frustration, melancholia, depression, apathy, lack of joy and enthusiasm for life, despondency. Mary's Thistle Golden Light Essence can also assist the regeneration of liver cells and protect against further liver damage.

The fun-loving, party, party, party *Dhanus* vedic sun sign person who loves the high living, good food, good wine and merrymaking can sometimes get too much of a good thing and come crashing down. It may be a tough life experience that brings them to the truth. Their constitution is vulnerable at the liver; they may need detoxifying and toning here. Mary's Thistle Golden Light Essence can help with this process to increase energy at the liver helping to carry away toxic substances and emotions, remove stagnation and bring back the positive energies of expansive Jupiter to their whole being in a more balanced way. The result is a feeling of more balanced joy which comes from within and which has a more permanent effect. As this feeling of joy becomes an inner experience which is not necessarily affected by outer circumstances, the *Dhanus* person becomes more established in the truth of their being and serene. This serenity and optimism is reflected to others by their very presence. This can have a very healing effect for them and for others that brings a sense of great achievement. To top it off their livers thank them too by not having to work so hard and feeling so much more comfortable. Access to pure joy becomes part of their natural state of being.

20. MEADOWSWEET GOLDEN LIGHT ESSENCE

(Fillipendula /Spiraeulmaria)
Major alterative to cleanse tissues.
Plant Family: Rosaceae (Rose).
Common Names: Queen of the Meadows,
Bridewort, Lady of the Meadow, Meadwort.
Parts Used: flowers, leaf, and whole plant in flower.

Keywords: *I turn remorse into sweetness.*

Meadowsweet Golden Light Essence is excellent for heartburn, reflux, gastritis, peptic ulcers, and dyspepsia. It may be taken in 5 drop doses twice daily for about 3 weeks. It soothes the stomach lining and heals the small intestine so that nutrients can be better absorbed into the bloodstream. Meadowsweet cleanses the blood of toxins and impurities. It can act here like having a "blood transfusion". Fevers, the pain of arthritis and rheumatism, gout and many "blood carried" diseases are relieved. Even young babies and children who may suffer reflux, vomiting, fevers and gastritis can be given Meadowsweet Golden Light Essence which will relieve these symptoms very quickly and effectively.

As *Kanyas* are sensitive in the stomach and small intestinal areas of the body, meadowsweet is a specific alterative or blood cleanser for them. It also calms the nervous system, relieving tension headaches, oedema, colds and fevers, "making the heart merrie and joyful and delighteth the senses" (John Gerard 1597). It brings sweetness to the whole being.

Kanyas are soothed and cleansed by the elegant white meadowsweet flower (plant) with its sweet almond scent. Their desire for perfection can bring tension, qualms of conscience at perceived indiscretions and remorse, which leaves a sour taste long after the event, is forgotten by everyone concerned. Symptoms of burning pains in the stomach and small intestine, heat in the head, face, joints and disturbed sleep can be the result. Water swelling in the tissues, urinary tract infections, and fevers may result. Meadowsweet Golden Light Essence can balance the PH of the tissues, soothe tension and tightness of the muscles of the neck and shoulders and ease pain and spasms. It can "teach" the over striving *Kanya* that there is value in Being as well as Doing and that perfection is always present in the here and now. They can experience true relaxation as the sweetness returns to their day to day lives.

21. MISTLETOE GOLDEN LIGHT ESSENCE

(Viscum album)
Major alterative to cleanse tissues.
Plant Family: Loranthaceae/Viscaceae
Common Names: Birdlime, Herb de la Croix,
Lignum Crucis, Mistel, Golden Bough, All Heal.
Parts Used: twigs, leaves, flowers, berries.

Keywords: *I make dreams a reality -
sacred herb of the Druids - contacting the dreaming for healing.*

Mistletoe Golden Light Essence enables you to contact the "dreaming"
– the collective unconscious for bringing dreams into reality and for
healing deep seated family issues and conflicts. It is said to unlock
the mysteries of immortality and unconditional love for oneself and
others. It cleanses the nervous system and helps us cope with rapid
change and transformation in the coming new Golden Light Age.

People needing Mistletoe Golden Light Essence can have over-powering
insights into humanity and its suffering which they often find needless.
"If only humans could embrace universal brotherhood/sisterhood love
for each other," they say. Often they see love as not "personal" but
universal. This attitude can make them feel resentful towards authority
and a little "cool" towards their loved ones. Mistletoe Golden Light
Essence can bring comfort to their strained nervous systems and
irritated blood vessels. It can help them through periods of rapid change
and transformation and give them insight to overcome any obstacles
to personal and spiritual growth on both physical and psychological
levels. It can "show" them what they need to "see" to overcome daily
problems from the aspect of unconditional love and tolerance. Mistletoe
supports their oversensitive immune systems so that they can cope
better with toxins in the environment of our ever changing world of
rapid technological growth. It also helps to protect them psychically
from unwanted "parasites" in the spiritual world and astral planes.
Mistletoe Golden Light Essence helps the oversensitive (*Kumba*) *person*
to gain composure again and brings a higher understanding about the
underlying reasons for human suffering.

22. MUGWORT GOLDEN LIGHT ESSENCE

(Artemisia vulgaris)
Major nervine to pacify Vata
Plant Family: Compositae/Asteraceae
Common Names: Felon herb, Nagadamani
(Sanskrit), Ai ye (Chinese).
Parts Used: aerial parts, leaves, flowers.

Keywords: *I calm the moon energy. The sacred feminine.*

Mugwort is the herb of Artemis, the Greek goddess of the moon, the hunt and the feminine aspect of our beings. Mugwort Golden Light Essence heals the nervous system when it is agitated by an imbalance of the moon energies. It is used to aid childbirth, bring on menstruation, heals the pain associated with many complaints of the "female" psyche in both women and men. Mugwort eases the insomnia of a too active and vivid dream life which may disturb sleep. It helps to tone the nervous system and protects the aura during "out of body" experiences.

Kumba people needing Mugwort Golden Light Essence can have very acute sensitivity to light and to sensory stimulation generally. They can suffer from insomnia, nightmares, sleepwalking and sleep so lightly that any little noise disturbs them. They can be so highly strung that their brains never switch off completely. This puts a lot of stress on their nervous systems. They can be very absent minded, "spaced out" and just can't concentrate or relax brain activity. They have an enormous need for solitude and silence, often seeming to be very anti-social to their friends and loved ones. The five senses of sight, smell, taste, hearing and touch are often overwhelmed by the intensity of their feelings and emotions. They can appear vague, at times even being absent for a second or two (petit mal?).

Mugwort Golden Light Essence can help to ground them in the here and now and helps to repair their "gapped" nerve fibres. This brings them into the reality of their physical bodies and helps keep them in touch with looking after their health needs.

23. OATS GOLDEN LIGHT ESSENCE

(Avena sativa)
Major nervine to pacify *Vata*.
Plant family: Graminaceae (Grains).
Common Names: Groats, Oatmeal, Hafer, Oat straw.
Parts Used: seeds, and whole plant in flower.

Keywords: *I act. I give strength to muscles.*

Oats are very healing to the nervous system for people recovering from debilitating illness, fevers, nervous exhaustion and gastro-intestinal inflammation. The herb Oats is also used to heal shingles and herpes infections which travel along nerve endings. It soothes the bladder and tissues of the kidneys and reproductive organs.

The Oats (*Mesha*) person picture is one of action. They often act first and think later. They can be spontaneous, impatient to get things done and hungry for interesting, often adventurous life experiences. They may have a strong, large frame and in good health, they are energetic and fit. Sometimes they may be top athletes in endurance sports. All this effort can put stress on their nervous systems, muscles, hearts and blood vessels and they can go into overdrive which may cause nervous and muscular fatigue and atrophy. Nerves and muscles may get tense and they may find it harder and harder to relax these adrenalin saturated muscles. They may suffer from insomnia. They may start looking a bit saggy and weak – help, we must bring back that basic *Meesha* sun sign energy of action, alertness, spontaneity, endurance and resilience.

What better way than to give Oats Golden Light Essence. The whole nervous system is pacified and balanced. *Mesha* may now feel the balance between exertion and relaxation. "What a relief! Love that porridge for breakfast. Better take a few muesli bars on my next hike". Well off again onto the next adventure for the positive *Mesha*, as their sun energy shines again.

24. PASSIONFLOWER GOLDEN LIGHT ESSENCE

(Passiflora incarnate)
Major nervine to pacify *Vata*.
Plant Family: Passifloraceae.
Common Names: Grandilla, Passion Vine,
Maracoc, Maypops.
Parts Used: aerial parts – flowers, leaves, and stems.

Keywords: *I calm the passions.*

Passionflower Golden Light Essence can ease headaches, palpitations in heart, nervous exhaustion, insomnia, spasms in digestive system, high blood pressure, cough, asthma, colic, haemorrhoids, muscle pains, intestinal inflammation. It can heal pelvic congestion and period pains by its antispasmodic action. Persistent insomnia can be relieved, even for very small babies and children as it acts on the sleep centre of the brain. Any emotional confusion is clarified by giving deep spiritual insights. The heart and throat chakras are attuned to higher spiritual levels of consciousness. Passions are calmed. The spirit of passionflower mirrors the divinity embodied by Jesus, of compassion and unconditional love for all of God's creation. The *Vrishika* Vedic sun sign person can often be an intense ball of energy, so passionate about life that it wears them out. They often have a great need to withdraw completely and often suffer bouts of complete insomnia. The soothing action of Passionflower can help us to let go of the cares and worries of the day so that we can drift off into a calm and deep sleep, waking up refreshed, ready to face what the next day may bring.

Passionflower Golden Light Essence eases the transits of Chiron and so supports the death and rebirth cycle of transformation, which is so much a part of the energy of *Vrishika*. Jittery, nervous states, which are often part of the experience of death/rebirth and transformation, are eased and the nervous system is renewed and strengthened. Intense dream states are clarified and nightmares are eased. Emotional states are pacified and new energies are gradually unfolded with greater positive spiritual understanding. Passionflower releases any guilt and difficulties with personal power issues, allowing the discovery of Christ Love to permeate the physical body. The intense ball of *Vrishika* energy is transmuted to waves of unconditional love.

25. PEONY GOLDEN LIGHT ESSENCE

(Paeonia spp.)
Major tonic to rejuvenate tissues.
Plant Family: Ranunculaceae.
Common Names: Paeony, Red Peony (*Chi Shao*), White Peony (*Bai Shao*) , Mountain Peony (*Mu Dan Pi*), Pfingstrose (German).
Parts Used: flowers, seed, roots, leaves and stems.

Keywords: *The spiritualization of sexual love.*

Peony Golden Light Essence treats fevers, swellings, pains from traumatic injuries, night sweats, and muscular spasms (especially in the bowel and reproductive organs). Peony can clear obstructions in the bowel, menstrual cramps, tension and nervousness. It can help to open us up to our own intuition and a knowing of our own inner divinity. The third eye chakra (sixth) is activated so that we can know and express our inner knowledge outwardly. Issues of sexuality and power are balanced. Peony is ruled by Pluto and the Sun so that dark, inner mysteries are revealed and brought into the light.

The Vedic sun sign of *Vrishika* rules the bowel and reproductive areas in the physical body. The *Vrishika* person, ruled by the mysterious, dark, transformative powers of Pluto, lord of the underworld, often feels overcome by these strong energies. Pluto leads us to the "dark night of the soul", bringing death of the old, used up energies and leading us to the transformative powers of complete renewal of body, spirit and soul. During this midnight passage, the soul needs new strength, insight and protection and a vision of light for the journey ahead. The sometimes dark powers of sexuality need to be spiritualized to include the power of unconditional love for ourselves and others. The feminine energy of nurturing and caring for the self needs activation. Inhibitions and shyness need to make way for a true feeling of self-esteem.

Peony Golden Light Essence can bring the energy of beauty, light and grace. The *Vrishika* can safely come out of hiding to express his/her real self to the world. The false persona melts away in the divine light of faith in the Self.

26. PLANTAIN GOLDEN LIGHT ESSENCE

(Plantago major/minor)
Major tonic to rejuvenate tissues.
Plant Family: Plantaginaceae.
Common Names: Leaf of Patrick, Patrick's
Dock, Snakeweed, Ripple Grass, Cuckoo's Bread,
Englishman's Foot, Waybread, White Man's Foot,
Snigdhajira (Sanskrit), Ribwort.
Parts Used: whole plant in flower, and seeds.

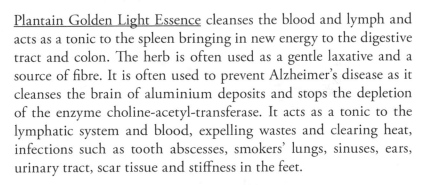

Keywords: *Moving into bliss.*

Plantain Golden Light Essence cleanses the blood and lymph and acts as a tonic to the spleen bringing in new energy to the digestive tract and colon. The herb is often used as a gentle laxative and a source of fibre. It is often used to prevent Alzheimer's disease as it cleanses the brain of aluminium deposits and stops the depletion of the enzyme choline-acetyl-transferase. It acts as a tonic to the lymphatic system and blood, expelling wastes and clearing heat, infections such as tooth abscesses, smokers' lungs, sinuses, ears, urinary tract, scar tissue and stiffness in the feet.

Meena rules the feet. So does the herb Plantain. So what better tonic for those sensitive Meena folk, with sore feet from treading the earthly path when they would much rather be in the water swimming around like fish, than Plantain Golden Light Essence. Plantain draws out toxins and heat, expelling them via the blood, colon, lymph and feet. It also draws up earth energy via the feet into the heart and head, bringing a renewal of spirit to the weary *Meena*. Old wounds are healed, blood and lymph are renewed. The soles of the feet receive a rejuvenating energy. *Meena* can move ahead again with more confidence, walking their earth path with material and spiritual abundance and a knowing that they are on the right path for them. This inner knowing brings great relief to them and gives them the insight to accept all of life's experiences as positive learning opportunities. This means that they can open their hearts to compassion and understanding without feeling that they must sacrifice a part of themselves to do so. What great life freedom comes to them!

27. RED CLOVER GOLDEN LIGHT ESSENCE

(Trifolium)
Major alterative to cleanse tissues.
Plant Family: Fabaceae (pea).
Common Names: Purple Clover, Cow Grass,
Trefoil, Vanamethika (Sanskrit).
Parts Used: flowering tops and leaves.

Keywords: *I bring Luck. I heal cysts.*

Red Clover Golden Light Essence can be used for cleaning up the lymphatic system, especially cyst formations. It is an excellent blood cleanser for weak patients and those suffering from cancer. Externally it is a good wash for cystic acne and dry, scaly skin. Its copper content and associated anti-spasmodic action makes it an excellent remedy for coughs, whooping cough and bronchitis. The flowers are an excellent estrogenic tonic for women and the leaf for men with prostate problems. Red clover is said to bring good fortune in all ways- health, wealth, luck, happiness and spiritual renewal. It also has a cleansing action on the spiritual and psychic properties of the blood and lymph, calming panic and hysteria. Red Clover Golden Light Essence may be taken in 5 drop doses, two times daily for cyst formation in the ovaries, neck and throat, breasts and pelvic inflammatory conditions.

The *Vrishika* Vedic sun sign person often appears to be very private, secretive and very sensitive to the atmosphere and "vibes" around them. They need their private space away from the influences of others quite often. They also have the tendency to hang on to everything, even their wastes and can therefore have troubles with constipation, walling off wastes into little sacs (cysts), and burying the effects of disturbing emotions in lymph and blood. Red clover can help to cleanse these toxic substances from their system, bringing a renewed sense of positivity and psychic protection from negativity within themselves and from others. It can act as a balancer, so enhancing the *Vrishika* ability to stay centred in their inner truth. Red Clover

<u>Golden Light Essence</u> also calms tension, panic and spasms of pain and discomfort, easing headaches, insomnia, thirst, irritated mucous membranes, hay fever, and sore throats. The colour red relates to the base chakra and has a cleansing and energizing effect here. Any fears and anxieties associated with survival and earning a living, emotional and material security, and energy renewal are calmed.

28. ROSEMARY GOLDEN LIGHT ESSENCE

(Rosmarinus officinalis)
Major tonic to rejuvenate tissues.
Plant Family: Lamiaceae (mint family).
Common Names: Dew of the Sea, Sea Rose, Polar Plant,
Mary's Mantle, Herb of Remembrance, Incensier.
Parts Used: whole flowering plant.

Keywords: *I reveal the mysteries of the Divine Feminine. I heal pain in the emotional body.*

<u>Rosemary Golden Light Essence</u> is a powerful antioxidant and has a tonic action on the circulatory system, relieving inflammation and protecting the capillary walls. It prevents hardening of the arteries and heart disease. It also improves blood circulation to the brain, preventing memory loss and hair loss. It is a rejuvenating tonic for all female ailments, nervous stress, headaches, palpitations, strokes, loss of speech, indigestion, muscle pain, and strengthens the sight. Brew a tea to lift heavy emotional states and to bring mental clarity. Rosemary is an excellent herb to use around childbirth to cleanse and strengthen the womb and the motherly, nurturing abilities. It is a symbol of marital love and fidelity and brings the Divine Mother healing and nurturing. Rosemary lifts the veil of illusion and gives us the memory of the mysteries of the divine feminine. It links us to the consciousness of Mother God.

The vedic sun sign of *Kataka* is ruled by the moon and the mother energy. Sometimes people born under this sign can find this moony, mothering energy just too much. They can then close off to the nurturing energy of Mother-God and feel quite disoriented both physically and spiritually.

<u>Rosemary Golden Light Essence </u>can help them find their 'polar star" centre again, reconnecting the incarnated spirit to the earth mother and Divine Mother healing energies. Then "mothering" becomes easier for both themselves, and for others. They reconnect

with their innate deep empathy and compassion for themselves and others. Their "moony" emotional energy and subtle body is more balanced and receptive. They are uplifted and energized. The heart energy is restored and toned. They start to remember to call upon the nurturing and supportive energy of the Divine Mother once again. Life starts to flow, flow, flow again.

29. SARSPARILLA GOLDEN LIGHT ESSENCE

(Smilax officinalis)
Major alterative to cleanse tissues.
Plant Family: Liliaceae.
Common Names: Red-bearded Sarsparilla,
Bamboo Briar, Dwipautra (Sankrit), Tufu ling (Chinese).
Parts Used: roots, flowers and leaves.

Keywords: *I bring balance to hormones.*

Sarsparilla Golden Light Essence as a detoxifying and balancing action on the liver, adrenals and reproductive organs. Tulas often need cleansing and balancing in these areas. They may suffer from chronic hormonal problems, acne, period pain, rheumatic pains, skin problems and infertility issues.

Tulas need balancing in all the paired organs – kidneys, adrenals, thyroid/parathyroid ovaries, testes, lungs. Sarsparilla Golden Light Essence can be used for this purpose. It is often used for hormonal balance in the liver, which may show as physical symptoms such as acne, absence of period, low sperm count, infertility, menopausal hot flushes and chronic low adrenal energy. Thyroid hormone imbalance may show as dry skin, hair loss, joint pain, poor metabolism and weight gain/loss. Bones may calcify abnormally, causing rheumatism and arthritis and even gout. Sugar balance may be disturbed. Migraines may result from hormonal fluctuations.

Tulas can come back into balance, finding it easier to make decisions in daily life without feeling guilt. The nervous system is pacified and the heat dispersed. Mental agonies and emotional disturbances are eased. Ying and Yang are balanced and new energy can flow into all the paired organs mentioned above. Venus and Jupiter – beauty and expansion of consciousness –are renewed and balanced. Love rules again.

30. SKULLCAP GOLDEN LIGHT ESSENCE

Scutellaria lateriflora
Major nervine to pacify *Vata*.
Plant Family: Lamiaceae.
Common Names: Mad Dog Weed, Virginian Scullcap,
Blue Pimpernel, Hoodwort, Helmet Flower. Chinese –
S.baicalensisor Huang Qin.
Parts Used: leaf, flowers and root.

Keywords: *I give stamina to your spinal nerves.*

Muscle spasms, insomnia, emotional disturbances of anger, hatred, jealousy, arthritis, headaches in skull region, tremors, convulsions, neuralgia, neurosis, premenstrual cramps, hypertension, depression, palpitations, urinary incontinence, fevers, strokes, addictions, high cholesterol, disorders of the central nervous system can be treated with Skullcap Golden Light Essence.

Maithuna vedic sun sign folk or people needing Skullcap crave lots of mental stimulation as they love new challenges and life experiences. Their minds often leap from one idea to another and if they are not mentally stimulated, they can become agitated and irritable, self-pitying or even cruel. They hate boredom. These ideas and mental energy often need "grounding" and balancing. The energy of Saturn helps to bring these dreamy ideas into reality. It gives *Maithunas* the energy to "follow through" and see real results. It gives stamina to their nervous systems. Skullcap is ruled by the planet Saturn which is often seen as the hard task master but can bring the positive energy of "earthing" dreams and ideas into positive, physical reality. Too much mental activity can bring imbalances in the adrenal glands and lead to "burnout" or nervous exhaustion. Emotional "ups and downs" result and adrenal collapse may follow. Skullcap Golden Light Essence can help to restore this imbalance and calm the "highly strung" *Maithuna*. People needing Skullcap can often have a characteristic triangulated upper eyelid, which droops at the corner of the eye. Tension headaches, migraines and congestion in the head area are common symptoms for these folk. Healing and nervous system resilience can return with this essence. Adrenal hormones are restored and the neuro-endocrine system is again in balance. Peace and relaxation return to the mind and emotions. Conflicts are resolved. *Maithunas* are now ready to take on new life challenges with a calm and balanced disposition.

31. SUNFLOWER GOLDEN LIGHT ESSENCE

(Helianthus annus)
Major tonic to rejuvenate tissues.
Plant Family: CompositaeAsteraceae.
Common Names: Corona Solis, Solo Indianus,
Marigold of Peru, Chimalati.
Parts Used: flowers and seeds.

Keywords: *I balance the Solar Plexus. The Gold of the physical and spiritual Sun. The Centre of the Circle.*

For poor circulation, digestive disturbances (imbalances in the solar plexus chakra), poor assimilation of fats, strengthens the heart, Sunflower eases rheumatism, strengthens a weak spine and repairs discs; for weak eyes, fingernails, hair and skin, coughs, colds and bronchitis. Sunflower Golden Light Essence may be used for fevers, malaria, eczema, kidney and bladder problems and as a diuretic. It eases sunburn. It balances spiritual leadership in the personality and brings the quality of light and compassion to the soul. Sunflower helps us to shine our spiritual light (sun) both within and without in a balanced way which brings blessings to all.

*Simba*s ruled by the Sun, the element of fire and is a masculine energy relating to the Father. *Simbas* are natural leaders and when positive, can shine like the sun, bringing warmth and heart-felt love to all just as the sun shines on us all. The sunflower is a symbol of light and warmth and positive personal power that comes from the inner Self and a deep connection via the solar plexus and the sacred heart with the divine will. The Sunflower Golden Light Essence brings the golden energy of the sun into our lives and gives courage to the heart. Sometimes *Simbas* need balancing at the solar plexus and the heart energy needs strengthening. They can have a tendency to be haughty, arrogant and vain or lacking in self-esteem and self-confidence. Positive attitudes of fathering and experiences of fathering help to balance this issue of self-confidence. *Simbas* are born leaders and need a balanced ego to bring positive energy to leadership and to bear the emotional ups and downs of love and hate; glory and shame. The Sunflower Golden Light Essence energy can promote the awareness that "One is All and All is One."

32. VALERIAN GOLDEN LIGHT ESSENCE

(Valeriana officinalis)
Major nervine to pacify *Vata*.
Plant Family: Valerianacea.
Common Names: Phu, All-heal, Amantilla, Baldrianwurzel, Herb of the Cats, Tagara (Sanskrit), St. George's Herb.
Parts Used: flowers and roots.

Keywords: *All heal.*

<u>Valerian Golden Light Essence</u> may be used in 5 drop doses, twice daily to relax the smooth muscles of the body and bring about relief from pain and insomnia. The flower essence may be used to pacify the emotions of anger, excitability, hysteria, nervous breathlessness, neuralgia and hyperactivity. Cramps and intestinal disorders leading to congestion in the liver and irritable bowel can be relieved with valerian. Congestion in the blood vessels and in the reproductive system may be eased, especially where the nerves are tense from the emotion of suppressed anger.

Simbas can sometimes be overly controlling, perfectionist and rather cool emotionally as they try to hide the vulnerability of their big and generous hearts. They may push themselves to the limit of nervous system endurance and their muscles will become very tense. Tension, tension, tension all over! How can they trigger the body to start the process of relaxation? The body cannot maintain nervous and muscle tension constantly. It is as if the sympathetic and parasympathetic nervous systems are confused. Anger builds up. The *Pitta dosha* becomes deranged and excess heat builds up in the liver and other organs, including the skin. The blood vessels suffer. There is venous engorgement and even the heart may be under strain. They just can't relax and are almost too afraid to let go enough to relax, for if they do the pain comes on. As relaxation comes, so does the pain appear, as the tense nervous and muscular fibres retract. This pain can bring on migraines, headaches, stomach pain, chest pain, pelvic pain. Pain flits and flies all over the body. <u>Valerian Golden Light Essence</u> can be very helpful to trigger the relaxation process and to sedate the resulting pain. The *Simba* sun can shine calmly and brightly again.

33. VERVAIN GOLDEN LIGHT ESSENCE

(Verbena officinalis)
Major nervine to pacify *Vata*.
Plant Family: Verbenaceae.
Common Names: Herb of Grace, *Eisenkraut*,
Holy herb, Herb of the Cross, Herb of Venus.
Parts Used: flowers, leaves, stems.

Keywords: *Messenger of Peace and Devotion – BEING.*

Vervain is used traditionally to drive away bladder stones and to balance calcium in the body. It is used in formulas for liver and gallbladder complaints and chronic skin conditions; for neuralgias and hormonal headaches; to heal bleeding wounds and spongy gums. It is a nerve tonic, helping insomnia and digestion. Vervain has also been used to treat various growths (cancers) of the neck, spleen and reproductive organs. Vervain is one of the Bach Flower remedies used for people who stress their nervous systems by their over striving and fanaticism about a cause. It helps people to practice moderation and tolerance; to ground their idealism. When the fiery light of Vervain radiates through the body and the physical world, it becomes more luminous and contained, giving the soul the energy to be able to inspire, lead and heal ourselves and others. Vervain Golden Light Essence can be used in five drops doses, twice daily to help heal this symptom picture and bring you into the positive energy of devotion and grace.

Kanya folk often find themselves stressed from over conscientiousness and over enthusiasm for an ideal of perfection in life. They find it almost impossible to relax and rest until everything they have thought of doing for that day, is *done.* They often make unrealistic lists of tasks for a given time period and must finish everything on the list before they can unwind. So they often feel great tension in the nervous system and their nerves, muscles and ligaments become tight and tense. They get aches and pains all over the place, itchy skin and eyes, bladder and bowel problems (no time to go), headaches and neuralgias. <u>Vervain Golden Light Essence</u> can help these stressed Kanya folk to be more realistic in the demands they make on themselves and others. They can't stop making lists but they can make the lists more realistic, so that they can relax at the end of the day as they have ticked off everything on their prioritized, shortened, daily list. Their minds and bodies are then able to relax, unwind and come to rest at last as they have finished their tasks.

34. VIOLET GOLDEN LIGHT ESSENCE

(Viola odorata)
Major alterative to cleanse tissues.
Plant Family: Violaceae.
Common Names: Sweet/ Blue Violet, Common Violet.
Parts Used: whole plant- leaves, flowers and stems.

Keywords: *I calm anxiety.*

VIOLET LEAF

<u>Violet Golden Light Essence</u> may be used for anxiety and panic attacks and to cleanse the lymphatic and nervous systems in people who are overcome by shyness. The cleansing action on the lymph makes violet leaf an excellent remedy for cold, coughs, tonsillitis, ear infection and lymphatic swellings. As a strong alterative/blood cleanser, violet leaf can be used to strengthen the immune system in many forms of cancer involving the lymphatic system. <u>Violet Golden Light Essence</u> can be taken in 5 drop doses, twice daily for about three weeks to bring you into the positive energy of healing this symptom picture.

Our dear, sweet, sensitive, watery *Meena* folk can suffer profound shyness in social situations. They can have real fears about losing their boundaries and identity in group situations and in day to day living in this harsh "earthly" plane. They tend to retreat from life, nervous and timid of others to the point of appearing aloof which brings them isolation and loneliness. <u>Violet Golden Light Essence</u> can help to calm this anxiety and panic and give them the support to assert themselves in a positive way with others. It can help to bring out their intuitive and spiritual natures so that they feel more confident to use these skills in feeling compassion for themselves and others. It can strengthen their immune systems and helps to protect their boundaries so that their systems do not pick up on toxicity around them. If they allow their personal boundaries to be ill-defined, guilt and resentment may build up to the point where the *Meena* person turns completely and loses all sense of compassion for themselves and others. "What has happened to this sweet violet?"

their loved ones wonder. They may turn into a "selfish monster" in an effort to protect themselves from "merging" with others and losing their identity completely. <u>Violet Golden Light Essence</u> can surround them with the protection they need. What a relief!

35. YARROW GOLDEN LIGHT ESSENCE

(Achillea millefolium)
Major alterative to cleanse tissues.
Plant Family: Compositae/Asteraceae.
Common Names: Soldier's Herb, Herba Militaris, Schafgabe (German), Bloodwort, Nosebleed, Thousand Leaf, Woundwort, Ichi Kao (Chinese), Gandana (Sanskrit).
Parts Used: stems, leaves, flowers, and seeds - whole herb.

Keywords: *I heal the deepest wound of the Heart.*

When the over-conscientious, success driven, hardworking *Mesha* person goes into burnout and feels disconnected in their relationships to others, heat builds up in the blood and the circulatory system starts to suffer. There is contraction in the blood vessels, which leads to spasms and pain. The nervous system also suffers from burnout, inflammation and subsequent pain. Yarrow Golden Light Essence can help this person slow down and reconnect to the feeling element of being. In 5 drop doses, twice daily, it can act to eliminate toxins from the blood and colon and heal the deep wound to the heart which may have caused the original disconnected feeling from Self.

The Yarrow (*Mesha*) person is ruled by his head and the thinking function, which can result in conflict between head and heart (feeling function). There can be an over-striving in ambition and worldly achievements which can cause a build up of heat in the blood, leading to fevers, bleeding (nose, colon, uterus, gums and ulcers), inflammatory states of emotions, tissues and circulation. They may feel a sense of alienation from their true feelings or even not know what they feel. Trauma or stress may precipitate this state as they are often impatient in wanting to get things done and be successful in business. Eventually the heart may suffer, causing heart diseases, circulatory problems or angina. Yarrow Golden Light Essence can help the *Mesha* person to reconnect to the feeling element of being and to their inner soul world. It can also protect them from any physical or psychic dangers they may encounter as their being becomes more sensitive to a harsh environment around them. They can then "open their hearts" to compassion and self-less love more easily and feel protected. The head and the heart start to work in unison once again.

36. YELLOW DOCK GOLDEN LIGHT ESSENCE.

(Rumex crispus)
Major alterative to cleanse tissues.
Plant Family: Polygonaceae
Common Names: Curled Dock, CommonDock,
Narrow Dock, Sour Dock, Amla Vetasa (Sanskrit).
Parts Used: roots, seed, leaf and flowers.

Keywords: *I clear heat from the liver.*

Skin eruptions and itchiness, liver congestion (heat), tickling cough in upper throat, dysentery/constipation, nervous irritability, palpitation, shock, emotional rancour, trauma, falls, pride, piles and bleeding, jaundice, stomach acidity, cancer, necrosis of tissues and anaemia all come under the healing influence of <u>Yellow Dock Golden Light Essence</u>. Its laxative action clears toxins from the bowel and frees up the liver energy. It can be used for jaundice and bilious complaints in the gastro intestinal tract and clears the bile flow in the gallbladder. Yellow dock is often included with other herbs in the treatment of necrosis and some cancers and glandular swellings. It may be used as a wash for chronic skin eruptions and thrush.

Simbas are ruled by the fiery, hot Sun and often have imbalances in the *Pitta dosha*, which may manifest as heat in the liver, blood and skin. The *liver Qi* may be blocked, producing poor energy flow and congestion in the solar plexus region. Emotional confusion and stagnation may result. These *Simbas* do not know how they feel about anything. They can't make decisions easily. They don't know what they want in life. They mistrust themselves and others. Their own intentions are unclear to them and to others. They find it difficult to make their way in the world. This is a very sorry state for anyone to be in, especially for the *Simbas*, who yearn to shine, shine, shine their sun energy. Anger and rancour arise. They feel "hard done by" and may get a chip on the shoulder. They often edit their emotions and feelings to appear acceptable to others.

<u>Yellow Dock Golden Light Essence</u>, ruled by Jupiter, can bring about an expansion of awareness and a balance of the sun energy in the *Simba* constitution. The blood is cleansed of accumulated toxins. The solar plexus and heart energies are pacified. Liver heat subsides. Fiery emotions are calmed and real feelings surface. The will of the divine is activated, bringing with it increased focus and clarity of the heart and mind working in unison. The *Simba* sun can shine again.

GINGER GOLDEN LIGHT ESSENCE

Ginger is used in Ayurvedic healing to rekindle the *agni* or the digestive fire. This is necessary to help burn out toxins in any panchakarma treatment as the digestive fire is often low. As toxins are released more fuel is needed to burn them out. You can take the <u>Ginger Golden Light Essence</u> for this purpose.

MARSHMALLOW GOLDEN LIGHT ESSENCE

Marshmallow is a herb which softens and draws out toxins from the cells and tissues. It is very protective and is used in this Ayurvedic Panchakarma treatment instead of butter Ghee (which can be very unpalatable) to soften and draw out the toxins prior to elimination with your suitable alterative or blood cleanser. This makes the whole process much more efficient and comfortable.

You use both these essences with your three personal vedic sun sign Golden Light Essences for Panchakarma Cleansing and Rejuvenation.

This makes a total of FIVE golden light essences for each Vedic Sun Sign personal detoxification and healing program which takes about 10 weeks to complete (about 2 weeks for each essence). At the end of this treatment you will vibrate very strongly on a spiritual and physical level with the Golden Light of Healing and the positive energy of your personal Golden Sun. You will notice this Golden Sun energy bringing many positive thoughts to your mind, rejuvenating your cellular structure and healing your physical body in a very gentle but powerful way. This Golden Light energy will also radiate out from you to others and to healing for Mother Earth and all her beings.

THE 36 GOLDEN LIGHT ESSENCES/ KEYWORDS.

1. **Alfalfa**	I reconnect you to the Great Cycle of Time.
2. **Burdock**	I remove the mask and show you your Self.
3. **Chamomile**	I calm any battle of wills and soothe digestion.
4. **Comfrey**	I unite. I make whole.
5. **Damask Rose**	Come into the inner cave of your own heart .
6. **Elderflower**	Fairy Magic. "The complete medicine chest."
7. **Fenugreek**	I bring increased nutrition to all cells.
8. **Gardenia**	I activate intuition
9. **Gentian**	I dispel doubt. I bring certainty.
10. **Golden Seal**	I give you renewed faith in your Divinity.
11. **Hops**	I turn shame into honour.
12. **Hypericum**	I heal nerve pain and bring in White Light.
13. **Hyssop**	I turn guilt into forgiveness.
14. **Iris**	I reconnect you to the rainbow bridge....
15. **Kelp**	Help I need some kelp. Source energy.
16. **Lavender**	I remove karmic blockages to spiritual growth
17. **Lemon Balm**	I lift your spirits.
18. **Lotus**	Jewel of Enlightenment. I bring purity.
19. **Mary's Thistle**	I heal the liver and bring JOY.
20. **Meadowsweet**	I turn remorse into sweetness.
21. **Mistletoe**	I help you contact the Dreaming for healing.
22. **Mugwort**	I calm the moon energy.
23. **Oats**	I help you get into action.
24. **Passionflower**	I calm the passions.
25. **Peony**	I spiritualize sexual love
26. **Plantain**	I get your feet moving – into Bliss.
27. **Red Clover**	I bring Luck. I cleanse the lymph.
28. **Rosemary**	I reveal the mysteries of the Divine feminine.
29. **Sarsparilla**	I bring balance to hormones
30. **Skullcap**	I give stamina to your spinal nerves.
31. **Sunflower**	I balance the solar plexus
32. **Valerian**	All heal. I bring health to nerves and liver.
33. **Vervain**	I bring peace, devotion and grace
34. **Violet Leaf**	I calm anxiety
35. **Yarrow**	I heal the deepest wound of the heart.
36. **Yellow Dock**	I heal the heat of rancour from the liver.
+ **Ginger**	I increase the fire energy of the digestion
+ **Marshmallow**	I soften and draw out cellular toxins.

You may use this list as a guide to choosing an essence to use for personal healing when you feel the need. Take 5 drops 2x day of the 15 ml dosage Golden Light Essence chosen till you finish the bottle.

USING THE GOLDEN LIGHT PLANT HEALING ESSENCES

Preparation and Dosage:

- You can make up dosage bottles from the Stock essences by taking a 15 ml bottle and adding 5 ml of brandy and 10 ml of purified water.
- To this you add FIVE drops of the Stock Golden Light Essence chosen.
- You then take FIVE drops twice daily internally straight from the bottle.
- If you only have access to the 15ml Stock bottles of the Golden Light Essences you can take these directly from the Stock bottle by putting FIVE drops in a little water and taking this two times daily.
- As the Golden Light Essences are vibrational healing essences either method is quite efficient and safe.
- The essences vibrate to the number 5 and the Golden Angels of the 5 elements for purification and deep karmic healing- safely and gently.

Ways to use the Golden Light Plant Healing Essences:
You can use any of the 36 essences as required for healing into wholeness or for a particular emotional or physical issue. Please see the general guide pages for further information on this. You can read the individual golden light essence descriptions above for further insights about the essences. You can also use the Divinatory Card Deck to divine a suitable **Golden Light Essence** for you to take at this time. You may like to use the Guided Meditations to meditate on your chosen Essence.

You can come into the positive energy of your Vedic sun sign using your personal Vedic sun sign essences (see Vedic sun sign chart for determining your personal vedic sun sign according to your date of birth.) The birth times for the vedic sun signs are different from the western sun signs. The golden light essences vibrate to these vedic times and can be used to do deep Panchakarma healing.

You can determine your Vedic Sun Sign here:

1. Your personal date of birth _____

2. Consult the Vedic Sun Sign Chart above.

3. According to the Vedic Sun Sign Chart I have the Vedic
   Sun Sign _____

   with the attribute of _____

4. My three personal Golden Light Essences are

   _____ (my nervine)
   _____ (my blood cleansing alterative)
   _____ (my rejuvenating tonic)

I must also take Ginger and Marshmallow Golden Light essences
as indicated above for all of the Vedic sun signs doing Panchakarma
detoxification and rejuvenation.

An example:

My date of birth is February 20th

According to the Vedic Sun Sign Chart I have the Vedic Sun Sign
of KUMBA with the personal attribute of INSIGHT.

My 3 personal Golden Light Essences are

MUGWORT (my nervine to pacify vata)
MISTLETOE (my blood cleansing alterative)
GARDENIA (my rejuvenating tonic)

This is an example of how a person with a **Kumba** Vedic sun sign does the 10 week PANCHAKARMA cleanse and rejuvenating treatment:

1. I take 15ml of *Mugwort Golden Light Essence* at 5 drops, twice daily until finished (about 2 weeks.)

2. I take 15ml of *Ginger Golden Light Essence* at 5 drops, twice daily until finished.

3. I take 15ml of *Marshmallow Golden Light Essence* at 5 drops, twice daily until finished.

4. I take 15ml of *Mistletoe Golden Light Essence* at 5 drops, twice daily until finished.

5. I take 15 ml of *Gardenia Golden Light Essence* at 5 drops, twice daily until finished.

Finish each essence before you go onto the next one.

This program will bring you into the positive energy of your personal Golden Sun, leaving you feeling very light and bright and resolving many personal Karmic emotional and physical issues in a gentle but powerful way. The Golden Angels of Healing and the Plant Kingdom of Mother Earth assist you in every way with this process.

To do your own personal Panchakarma healing select your Golden Light Essences for your Vedic Sun sign for your own birth date. Remember that each Vedic sun sign also needs Ginger and Marshmallow Golden Light Essences for this Panchakarma process. They are common to all the Vedic signs. You need FIVE Golden Light Essences for this Panchakarma treatment.

Happy Panchakarma healing…

Blessing to you from the Golden Angels of Healing and Mother Earth!

Chapter 7. 36 Golden Light Plant Essences Guided Healing Meditations

This is how you could use the meditations. First you can invoke help as follows:

"We invoke the Golden Angels of Healing, Mother Earth and all the Devis of the Plant Kingdom to be present with us now.

Pour your healing blessings upon us as we meditate on each of the 36 Golden Light Essences.

We thank you with great love and great respect.

So be it and so it is…"

Choose the Golden Light Essence you wish to meditate upon and read the guided meditation text a few times. Then sit quietly with the intention to meditate on this healing essence for a while. Whatever happens is just right for your healing at this time. You can also extend any healing you may receive to Mother Earth and to all Beings in love and joy from your heart centre.

If you have the meditation CD on the Golden Light Essences you can use that for your meditations…

Blessings to you!

1. ALFALFA GOLDEN LIGHT ESSENCE
Guided Healing Meditation. (see meditation CD).

Relax and let go the cares and worries of the day. Breathe out long...... breathe in long....... Focus on your breath in this way for a while.......

We travel to North Africa to Medea, the home of Alfalfa.....

We call in the feminine energies and the planet Venus...

Be with us now......

We call in the Divine Arab physicians of healing...... Be with us now......

Feel their presence....

Focus on your nervous system, especially the nerves along the spinal column...

See or feel the Alfalfa plant bringing healing energy to your nerves here....

Feel the relaxing and releasing along the spine or anywhere you feel tenderness, pain, tension..... Feel any tension or pain dissolving......

Meditate on this healing energy as it flows through your body ...

Thank you Alfalfa, Venus and Divine Arab healers....

Gently bring your awareness back to this room....... and when you are ready open your eyes ...... stretch your body....

You may like to reflect on your healing Alfalfa experience.

2. BURDOCK GOLDEN LIGHT ESSENCE
Guided Healing Meditation. (see Meditation CD).

Relax and let go of the cares and worries of the day....

Focus your attention on the breath..........

Scan your body for any tension or discomfort and breathe into these areas to release it............. Feel easy.......

We call in the power of the Great White Spirit, the planet of love and beauty, Venus and the <u>Burdock Golden Light Essence.</u>

Be with us now.......Feel their Presence........

We ask for a detoxification of our emotional body......

Let any uncomfortable emotions which may surface be cleansed by the burdock plant and the Great White Light of the loving and soothing Venus...........

Feel your blood being cleansed...........................

Feel your thoughts being cleansed.....Feel the protection of Venus and burdock at the third eye area...Feel any negativity being washed away and being replaced by positive, motivational thoughts and insights...Stay with this process for a while........... Meditate in the Great Silence....

Bring your awareness back to the room..... When you are ready, gently open your eyes.........

We thank the Great White Spirit, burdock and Venus for their healing..........

You may like to contemplate your experience for a while....

3. CHAMOMILE GOLDEN LIGHT ESSENCE
Guided Healing Meditation. (see Meditation CD).

Relax and prepare yourself for a meditation.............

We call in the Egyptian sun god RA.......

Be with us now...

Awaken us to the inner light of the sun.

Bring us the healing energy of the chamomile flower.

Kindle the inner fire, letting it burn gently and constantly.

Bring us soothing. Bring us equilibrium and harmony.

Bring us the comfort of your golden rays of light.......

Feel this golden light entering the pineal gland at the centre of your head.......

Feel the soothing energy at your brow...eyes...nose...mouth.... throat....bronchials.......chest...lungs...stomach...pancreas... colon.....

Feel the peace and harmony in your mental and emotional body.....

Meditate on this soothing peace and harmony for a while....

Thank you sun god Ra. Thank you *Chamomile* plant.

Gently bring your awareness back to the room.......to your physical body.........to your breath.............

You may want to contemplate your healing experience for a while.

4. Comfrey Golden Light Essence
Guided Healing Meditation. (see Meditation CD).

Relax and let go of any cares and worries of the day....Focus on the breath as you breathe out long and then let the lungs fill again naturally...........

We call on the mighty power of Saturn/Father God and the earth healing energies of the comfrey plant..... Be with us now........

Heal us with grace and ease ... Feel their presence with us now......

Mentally scan your body for any areas that feel tension or strain.... We gently call in the healing of comfrey to these areas....

Continue with this process until you feel totally relaxed and at ease......

We call in Saturn/Father God to give us any new knowledge and awareness we may need to solve any earthly problems we may have at this time........

Just let this process happen quite naturally and easily ....

Meditate in the Great Silence for a while......

We thank you Saturn/Father God and the comfrey plant for any healing awakening and rejuvenating energies we have been able to receive.

Gently bring your awareness back to your physical body and to the room.

Seal your chakras and aura with the cross of light in the circle of light for protection and grounding. When you are ready you can open your eyes and just sit quietly for a while.

5. DAMASK ROSE GOLDEN LIGHT ESSENCE
Guided Healing Meditation. (see Meditation CD).

We call in the healing energy of Venus, the damask rose and the divine love and protection of Mother Mary......

Please be with us now......Feel their presence......

We travel to Greece, to the palace of Aphrodite, Venus, goddess of love. In the palace gardens we are surrounded by the beautiful, soft, pink roses. Their sweet perfume wafts around us....What divine beauty...What divine love....

We enter the heart, our centre of mysticism and our soul connection to the Divine soul of all creation..... What peace, what harmony...

We see ourselves in the cave of the heart....

A still, small, glowing flame burns there. We are in this flame in the cave of our own hearts. We feel an awakening, an energy renewal in our whole being.

We feel a renewed connection to the circle of all life and to the sun energy of the Christos.

Golden, whitish light pours into the back heart chakra, filling us with love and light.

We come to perfect rest in our own hearts. Meditate on this for a while....

We thank all our divine helpers and the damask rose plant for our healing as we travel back to the here and now. We place a cross of light in a circle of light over our heart chakra for protection.

Gently we bring our awareness back to the room as we contemplate our healing experience.

6. Elderflowers Golden Light Essence
Guided Healing Meditation. (see Meditation CD).

Relax as you totally let go of any cares and worries ......

Open yourself to the possibility of deep healing and cleansing with the elder tree mother. We call upon the "Divine Mother" of healing, Venus, planet of love and beauty, and the healing energies of the elder tree. Be with us now......

Feel their presence......

They say: "Prepare yourselves for a deep letting go of anything that is no longer required – is not of service to your Highest Self..... Gently let it go....let the elder mother carry it away to be transmuted by the Great Golden White Light.......

Feel the golden white light entering at the crown chakra and filling your whole being with renewed energy...............

Stay with this process for a while...........

Feel your renewed strength and vigour.

Feel renewed self esteem and a belief in your innate healing powers.

Feel the inner knowing that you have the ability to overcome obstacles and power of love and wisdom within you to solve your daily problems of life."

We thank the "Divine Mother", Venus and the elder tree for their healing.

Slowly become aware of your physical body and senses again and when you are ready, open your eyes. You may like to contemplate your experience for a while.

7. FENUGREEK GOLDEN LIGHT ESSENCE
Guided Healing Meditation. (see meditation CD).

Relax as you release any physical or emotional tension in your body......Focus on the breath......let the breath flow in and out naturally.........

We travel to the Greek Islands, to the healing gardens and temple of Apollo, the sun god. *Fenugreek* surrounds us. We focus in on the 'three-angled' form of the corolla of the plant. It reminds us of the Holy Trinity – the wholeness of our being.

Apollo appears in all his glory and invites us to eat of the plant. We do so. We see the golden energy of the fenugreek reach our nervous system and penetrate the cells in our physical and spiritual bodies, restoring them to complete health and giving us a beautiful energy of peace and calm. Any negativity we may feel is transmuted into this golden light energy. We feel so whole, so complete, so peaceful and so nurtured. Stay with this feeling for a while.....

Apollo says: "Call on me for daily guidance about what foods and beverages to consume for optimal health and nutrition.

Call as often as you like. I will answer you with intuitive messages about what to eat and drink. "

We thank Apollo and the fenugreek plant for any healing we have been able to receive.

Soon we find ourselves back in the room again as we gently open our eyes. You may like to contemplate your experience for a while.

8. GARDENIA GOLDEN LIGHT ESSENCE
Guided Healing Meditation. (see meditation CD).

Relax as you let go of the cares of day. Feel your body softening…..
Breathe in…. hold…..Breathe out …..Continue like this for a while
at a pace that is comfortable for you……

We travel to India, to the temple of Ganesha, the elephant god.
Ganesha invites us to "hop on board" as he runs through the
forests to a clearing of flowering gardenia plants. We smell the
divine perfume of the white gardenia flowers….how exquisite….
how calming….

We focus on the area between our eyebrows….Feel the calming
effect of the gardenia fragrance …..

Ganesha appears……. You feel a soft, white gardenia flower fall on
your third eye area……..Ganesha says, "I clear all heat, fear and
strong emotions from this chakra between your eyebrows. May
you forgive and be forgiven for any negative karma you may have
a memory of from this life or any past lives. Let it go…Let it be
transmuted into golden light and love for yourself and others. Feel
calm and serene.

Feel the intuitive knowing that you are totally protected at all times
and in all ways……"

Stay with this experience for a while.

Thank you Ganesha, the golden light and the gardenia. When you
are ready, gently open your eyes and return to everyday awareness.

9. GENTIAN GOLDEN LIGHT ESSENCE
Guided Healing Meditation. (see meditation CD).

Relax and let go any tension in your body.... Focus on the breath as you let the breath 'breathe' you......Imagine yourself travelling to Southern Germany - to the Black Forest area. This is a powerful earth healing centre. You arrive in the centre of a large forest of fir trees. You sit in a clearing, surrounded by yellow gentians in flower as dusk descends and a new crescent moon appears in the night sky. You feel a soothing yet stimulating energy and a warm, pleasant feeling around your stomach and liver area. As you sit quietly taking in the healing energy, a sliding door opens in the ethers and you enter an old black forest farm house. An old wizard greets you. "Hello, I've been waiting for you. You have some old wounds to heal. Follow me if you want to heal them now..." If you answered yes to the good old wizard, follow him now. You enter a dimly lit room in the house which has all sorts of healing herbs and bottles on the shelves around the walls. The old wizard says, "I am the universal Alchemist. I transmute any doubts you may have about your own inner healing abilities into certainty. In this way you can heal your own physical, emotional and spiritual wounds and move forward into living in the present moment with certainty and trust in the positive inner unfolding of your true Self and your connection to divine love and protection. See this large cauldron in the centre of the room? It is filled with an ancient healing medicine called *theriac* which contains gentian and other secret healing herbs. Imagine anything you want to have healed now. Let it look like a brown ball of energy and place it in the transmutation cauldron. Watch the magic brew transmute it into a ball of golden white light which enters your solar plexus chakra. See your solar plexus chakra spinning gently like a golden wheel. Feel the healing warmth in your stomach area; feel it spreading throughout your whole body - this gentle, healing warmth. Stay with this feeling for a while..."

Gently bring your awareness back to the room.... as we return from the Black Forest to the here and now. We thank the wizard Alchemist and the gentian plant for any healing we have received. When you are ready, you may open your eyes and sit quietly for a while as you contemplate your gentian healing experience.

10. GOLDEN SEAL GOLDEN LIGHT ESSENCE
Guided Healing Meditation. (see Meditation CD).

Feel your body relaxing as you let go any tensions and cares of the day........Focus on your breath for a while......

We call in the healing energies of the golden seal plant and the North American Indian healing elders as well as White Eagle and the sun/star brotherhood and sisterhood. Be with us now.

Shine your spiritual Sun upon us bringing warmth and light to our tired minds and bodies.

Restore our faith in our own inner divine healing powers. Strengthen our immune systems and grant us divine protection.

Feel the golden seal plant cleansing your blood and lymph like detergent.

The plant devis and healing angels carry away any toxins and wastes to the golden light of the sun for purification and transmutation.

Feel the golden sun energy pouring into your solar plexus and the white light filling your throat chakra. Stay with this process for a while........

As you return your awareness back to your physical body and the room around us, remember to thank the golden seal plant, the Indian healers, White Eagle and the Star Brotherhood/Sisterhood for any healing we have been able to receive.

You may like to contemplate your experience for a while.

11. HOPS GOLDEN LIGHT ESSENCE
Guided Healing Meditation. (see Meditation CD).

Relax as you let go the cares of the day......

Breathe out long....let the lungs fill again naturally.......

Continue breathing like this for a while.

We call in the beneficial influences of the planet Mars to cleanse our bloodstreams of heat and toxins and to give healing energy to liver, kidneys and adrenals.......

We find ourselves travelling to Lemuria, the ancient land of agriculture and healing and land in a beautiful, lush, green garden with a crystal clear stream running through it. At one end is a pond and a gentle waterfall. We let the cool water flow over us as it washes away all negativity and toxins from our bodies, minds and souls..........

We emerge from the waterfall into the hop garden again. Two glistening fairies appear, carrying a large skipping rope made of hop vines. They invite us to skip and jump as they swing the strong hop vine rope. We skip, jump, hop...skip, jump, hop....letting all our cares, worries and problems melt into the Divine Plan of life.

All emotions of anger, shame and worry melt into joy, love hope and honour.

After a while the two fairies gather up the hop rope and bid us farewell as we thank them for our healing. They embrace us with love as they whisper to us - "Remember to honour yourself with love, joy and FUN. Follow God's plan for you and relax into life."

Thank you Mars, hops and fairies for your healing.....

Slowly we re-emerge into our physical bodies and this room. You may like to contemplate your experience for a while.

12. HYPERICUM GOLDEN LIGHT ESSENCE
Guided Healing Meditation. (see Meditation CD).

Relax and let go the cares of the day……….

Focus on the breath…..Feel the ease of the breath as it breathes you……

We call in the healing energy of St. John of God , White Eagle and the Great White Light Star Brotherhood…..

Please be with us now….. Feel their presence….

We call in the healing energy of <u>Hypericum Golden Light Essence</u>to drive away any negativity and evil both within and without.

Send your healing energy to us now dear plant of Light. Dispel and banish all darkness from our hearts and minds and bodies.

Focus on the heart area…..See or feel the great white Light as a flame in the sanctuary of your own heart. Watch this steady flame as it grows and grows, illuminating your whole being…..See this great white light streaming from your heart to the mother earth and to all her people….. Feel the great white Light entering your heart, healing your heart and moving from your heart to the whole world, sending healing light and love to all.

Meditate on this for a while…….

We thank our dear plant, St. John of God and White Eagle for the healing we have been able to receive.

Slowly bring your attention back to your physical body… to the room…..and when you are ready, gently open your eyes. ….

You may want to contemplate your experience for a while……

13. HYSSOP GOLDEN LIGHT ESSENCE
Guided Healing Meditation. (see Meditation CD).

Let us invoke the benevolent and healing energies of the planet Jupiter, and the element of FIRE for protection and purification, purging any negativity from the lungs, solar plexus and the emotional body; integrating any new awareness into the subtle and physical bodies.........Focus your attention on the incoming and outgoing breath for a while..............

Feel the calming and balancing action of the breath.....Feel the warming effect throughout the body......Feel any tension in your body easing......Feel the healing energy of the Hyssop plant.....

Does anyone or any situation arise which brings up the emotion of guilt for you? Do you feel you would like to invoke forgiveness for yourself around this issue or person? If so.......

We call in the expansive and protective energies of Jupiter to help us now........."Benevolent Jupiter, help me to release that part of me which angers me and makes me feel guilty when I think of ...... person or situation..... Purify me and protect me. Bring forgiveness to everyone involved.....

Bring relief of any tension or stress in our bodies..... Shine your light and love on all.......In full faith and trust.... So be it and so it is!

Gently integrate any new awareness you may have into all your chakras and energy bodies................

We thank you Jupiter and hyssop for your awakening and healing.

Balance all our chakras and protect them with divine light and love.

Gently bring your awareness back to your body and to the room....... open your eyes......

You may want to contemplate your experience for a while......

14. IRIS GOLDEN LIGHT ESSENCE
Guided Healing Meditation. (see Meditation CD).

Relax any tension or pain in your physical body as you focus on the breath effortlessly......

We travel to Mount Olympus near Athens, to a fertile grove surrounded by beautiful Iris flowers. Let's tune into the energy field of the iridescent Iris flower as it 'speaks" its story to us.

Focus on seeing a golden Iris flower in your third eye chakra......Feel the warmth and peace here....

The Greek god, Juno/ Jupiter, messenger of the gods descends from the heavens along the rainbow bridge of white light, carrying with him this golden iris. He sits amongst us, radiating iridescent rainbow light healing. He says: "I bring you, oh earthly people with 'feet of clay', healing, creativity and inspiration. I 'breathe' the breath of 'inspiration' into you.

Gently release any blocks you may have to trust, divine creativity and healing now and surrender to the divine white light in your third eye chakra. May you awaken to your own divine birthright and remember God's will and plan for you in this incarnation. May you put this plan into action. Let go of any perceived imperfections and frustrations you may have. You are a perfect image of the Divine Creator. Let your rainbow light shine for all to see...."

Feel the energy of transcendence, of harmony, purification and rejuvenation around the third eye chakra. Feel the awakening of new energy here..... Breathe in this energy for awhile...

We thank you Jupiter and the Iris flower and for our healing and awakening of the third eye chakra....Gently bring yourself back to the here and now..... Focus on your breath.....When you are ready, open your eyes.....and stretch your body.

You may want to contemplate or journal your experiences.

15. KELP GOLDEN LIGHT ESSENCE
Guided Healing Meditation. (see Meditation CD).

Feel your body relaxing as you let go any cares and tensions of the day......Focus on the breath and breathe slowly and naturally.

We call in the healing energy of the moon, the feminine, the mighty god of the sea, Neptune and the kelp plant.

Be with us now....... Feel their presence......

We ask that our thyroid and glandular system be cleansed and rejuvenated with your healing energies, bringing renewed energy from the Great Source of Light and Love.

Feel this healing and let it flow through you as you return to the Source.

Stay with this process for a while.......

Become aware of any new insights you may be receiving......

Centre on the throat chakra....

Feel it opening and clearing....Feel new greenish/blue light filling the throat chakra with new energy.

Feel your communication channels opening and clearing...

We thank the moon, the feminine, Neptune and kelp for any healing we have been able to receive.....

Gently bring your awareness back to the room....

When you are ready, open your eyes.

You may want to contemplate your experience for a while.

16. LAVENDER GOLDEN LIGHT ESSENCE
Guided Healing Meditation. (see Meditation CD).

Relax as you let go the cares of the day.....

Focus on the breath as it flows in and out with great ease......

We call in the healing powers of the lavender plant with its cleansing and soothing fragrance, the planet Mercury and Hermes the divine magician of healing..... Be with us now....

Feel their presence......

Imagine your nervous system throughout your body...

See or feel all the nerves of your body being cleansed and toned and rejuvenated..........

Stay with this process for a while.....

Feel the peace coming over you........

Focus your attention on the crown chakra.......

See or feel any tension in your head, neck and shoulders easing......

We ask that any karmic blocks which might stop our spiritual development be taken away now........

Feel the release......Feel the new space and freedom.....

Meditate on this for a while.....

Return to your physical body and to the room around you......We thank the lavender and Mercury and Hermes for any healing we have been able to receive.....Gently open your eyes. You might like to contemplate your experience for a while....

17. Lemon Balm Golden Light Essence
Guided Healing Meditation. (see Meditation CD).

Relax and let any tension in your mind and body melt away.....

We call in the healing energies of the moon, the great ancient physician and healer Paracelsus and the lemon balm herb.

Be with is now........Bring your gentle, soothing but powerful healing to remove any melancholy or depression of spirits. Uplift our spirits and open our hearts to the healing power of grace. Bathe our hearts in the moon essence of tranquillity and peace. Calm our minds from anxiety and worry.

Visualize a pool of milk like a dish in the crown of your head.

Feel the soothing action this white milk has on your mind, brain, head and nervous system. Feel the milk overflowing from this "dish" into your body, bathing every cell with its rejuvenating energy.........

Stay with this process for a while........

Visualize this soothing, milky, lemon balm moon essence bathing the earth and all living beings in compassion and healing love.....

Feel the <u>Lemon Balm Golden Light Essence</u> entering and healing you ...... uplifting your spirit......Meditate on this for a while......

We thank lemon balm, the moon and Paracelsus for any healing we have been able to receive as we gently bring our awareness back to our body and the room.

Feel the grounding and protecting earth energies around you...

You may like to contemplate your experience for a while......

18. LOTUS GOLDEN LIGHT ESSENCE
Guided Healing Meditation. (see Meditation CD).

Let us invoke the Goddess Lakshmi who brings us spiritual and material abundance and prosperity.

Feel your mind being calmed and any restless thoughts subdued.

Focus your breath into your heart centre, opening yourself to devotion and unconditional love for yourself, all other living beings and the earth. Feel the purity of the Lotus flower enveloping all your subtle bodies, chakras, nadis and meridians......

Lakshmi appears in all her splendour. She says: "see the Golden lotus flower appear before you in the centre of your crown chakra. See the glowing jewel shimmering in its centre.........

Enter the jewel and feel the bliss of wisdom – of enlightenment.........

I give you this supreme gift. Receive it as you can.......Take this wisdom into your worldly life and use this Divine gift for solving any problems you may have. Know that I am with you and call on me for help anytime. Blessings to you, to all Living beings and to Mother Earth..."

Feel your own heart energy merging into the great Heart of the Divine consciousness and the heart of the Sun......Stay in this blissful energy of infinity and the triple 888 for a while......

Feel you own heart energy rejuvenated..... Let this process continue for as long as it needs to for you ......even over the next few days, weeks, months.....

Thanks be to you Divine Goddess Lakshmi and the Golden Lotus.

Gently become aware of your breath once more.

Feel your physical body and your surroundings.

19. MARY'S THISTLE GOLDEN LIGHT ESSENCE
Guided Healing Meditation. (see Meditation CD).

Relax as you release any tension in your body....

Focus on the breath.........

We call in the healing planetary angels of Mars, Saturn and Jupiter and the Mary's Thistle..... Be with us now....

Feel their presence with you now.......

We also call in Mother Mary to protect and heal us......

Feel Her mantle of protection and radiant light surrounding us at this time.

Focus on your right upper abdomen around the liver area....

Bringing in the healing energies we have just invoked, feel any changes or arising emotions and feelings as they come up for you....

Release them into the great fire of transformation and receive the purified energies in the form of the Great White Healing Light.

Stay with this process for a while......Meditate in the Great Silence.....

Thank you Mother Mary, Mary's Thistle and the Great White Healing Light and planetary energies of Mars, Saturn and Jupiter....

Gently bring your awareness back to your breath, your physical body and the room around you and when you are ready, open your eyes and breathe out and in deeply a few times to ground yourself.

Pati Solva Hueneke

20. MEADOWSWEET GOLDEN LIGHT ESSENCE
Guided Healing Meditation. (see meditation CD).

Letting go any tensions of the day and focusing on the breath as it gently moves in and out….lets travel tonight to a lazy summer's day by the banks of a gently flowing stream.

As we lie here, we are surrounded by the sweet smelling flowering meadowsweet plant and the Devis and nature spirits living in and around the plant who whisper their healing secrets to us……

Listen, listen carefully for a while……

Can you hear the messages…….?

Focus on the area of the small intestine in the lower abdomen…

Is there any tension or discomfort here?

We ask for the healing powers of the Meadowsweet plant to come to us now….

Please heal any dis-ease we may have here.

We focus on the blood coursing through our arteries and veins like a river of life. Meadowsweet please carry away any toxins and purify our blood………… Bring sweetness to all the tissues of our bodies……….

Stay with this process for a while…..

We thank the Meadowsweet and her Devis and nature spirits as we gently become aware of the room again.

Focus on the breath as you slowly open your eyes.

You may want to contemplate your experience for a while.

21. MISTLETOE GOLDEN LIGHT ESSENCE
Guided Healing Meditation. (see Meditation CD).

Relax and let go of any tension in your body........ Focus on the breath as you gently breathe out and in...............

We call in the energy of the sun god Apollo, the great Celtic druid priests and healers and the magical mistletoe plant. Be with us now.... Let us feel your presence......

Bring us your love and goodwill.......and healing.........

Focus on your nervous system.........

Feel the healing energy of the mistletoe cleansing, toning and repairing the nerves all over your physical and etheric bodies.......

Stay with this process for a while............

Focus on your spleen on the left upper abdominal area......

Feel the energy of mistletoe filling the back spleen with healing whitish-green golden light............

Meditate on this for a while....

We thank the mistletoe, Apollo and the druid priests for their healing......

Protect your chakras and aura with the cross of light in the circle of light and ground your energy....

Gently bring your awareness back to the room.........

You may want to contemplate your experience for a while...

22. MUGWORT GOLDEN LIGHT ESSENCE
Guided Healing Meditation. (see Meditation CD).

Let's travel to a place of Moon healing.......

We find ourselves in the Greek temple of Artemis, goddess of the moon. The temple is surrounded by deep woods and deer are roaming around peacefully......We hear an owl hooting......

The full moon shines brightly. There is a large fire burning.....

We sit in a grove of mugwort around a fire, watching and waiting.......

Artemis, the moon goddess appears, dressed in white and holding her hunting bow and arrow.....and silvery mugwort.....She speaks to us......"I am the guardian of the hunt......You and your loved ones are safe and spiritually protected........I am happy to assist you with healing all aspects of the feminine......I help you access your own inner moon wisdom..... Trust this inner wisdom and act on it without delay.....Quiet your mind and surrender all thought and worries to the loving, almighty power of the moon......

Closing your eyes, note the thoughts and feelings streaming into your consciousness........ Listen to your inner wisdom...Have faith... If you have disputes with others, ask me for guidance and wisdom to resolve them for the best of all concerned......and ask me for divine protection any time...."

Meditate for a while in the deep inner silence....

Slowly bring your awareness to your breath.... to the room

We thank the mugwort plant and the moon goddess for any healing we have received.

Seal all your chakras with a cross of light in a circle of light. Gently open your eyes...

23. OATS GOLDEN LIGHT ESSENCE
Guided Healing Meditation. (see Meditation CD).

Relax and let go the cares and worries of the day.

Focus on the breath...... breathe out long .... and inhale slowly.....

We call in the planets Venus and Mars to bring balance to our emotions and nervous system; balance to the feminine and masculine aspects of our psyche; balance to Yin and Yang; balance to exertion and relaxation in the muscles, ligaments and tendons.......

We call in the Tibetan Blue Medicine Buddha of Healing.....

We call White Eagle and the Great White Light Brotherhood/ Sisterhood......

We call in the Divine Pranic Healers.......

Be with us now..........

Bring the Oats Golden Light Essence healing to us in whichever way we need it at this time and in this space ......

Meditate on this healing energy for a while.......

Slowly bring your awareness back to the physical body..... to the room .....Gently open your eyes......... Focus on your breath again, breathing in and out naturally........

Contemplate your experience of the Oats Golden Light Essence healing for a while......

24. PASSIONFLOWER GOLDEN LIGHT ESSENCE
Guided Meditation. (see Meditation CD).

Allow your body to relax, completely letting go of the cares and worries of the day.

Breathe out…….. and in……..

Do this a few times……

Feel any tension in your nervous system dissolving away……..

We are travelling to Hawaii to an ancient Lemurian temple.

The temple gardens are surrounded by passionflower vines and we are greeted at the arched gate by five Lemurian priests who usher us into the sacred grove of the temple. Here we are anointed with <u>Passionflower Golden Light Essence</u>.

We inhale the sweet smell of the passionflower fragrance in the air.

We feel soothed and comforted.

Any nervous restlessness we may be feeling melts away. The heart chakra feels soft and gentle. The throat chakra feels relaxed. The Christ consciousness of pure, unconditional Love for ourselves and others enters us. We feel great *compassion* for ourselves and all other living beings. We ask that happiness and love may spread to all living beings and to the whole world.

We ask that all suffering may end, starting with our own suffering, We wish it to be transmuted into compassion and love.

Stay with this feeling for a while… Meditate in the deep silence…

Thank you passionflower, Christ consciousness and Lemurian priests… When you are ready, gently come back to everyday awareness.

25. PEONY GOLDEN LIGHT ESSENCE
Guided Healing Meditation. (see Meditation CD).

Relax your body, letting go of any tension…..

Focus on your breath coming in and out naturally……..

We call on the energy of the divine, Greek physician Asclepius, also known as "paeon" or helper…….

"Be with us now, Asclepius…………

Open our hearts and heal any wounds."

Our hearts are strong and can heal, can become whole again.

Feel any emotions which you may want to clear…….

Balance our heart chakra, Asclepius..

Peony, *Sho-yu*, most beautiful and graceful, heal us with your soothing, rejuvenating powers…….

Bring us the courage to dissolve away any false persona; to recognise our own inner Divinity and to present this Light of our own real Self to others and to the world around us with honesty and integrity and faith.

Meditate on this for a while….

Thank you with great respect and love. So be it and so it is….

Gently become aware of the room again and of your physical body…..
Breathe naturally…… Open your eyes……..

You may want to contemplate your experience for a while……

26. PLANTAIN GOLDEN LIGHT ESSENCE
Guided Healing Meditation. (see Meditation CD).

Relax and breathe easy...Let go of any concerns and worries...

We call in the planet Venus and the herb Plantain. Be with us now.....

Focus on your feet...

Feel if there is any pain, tension or tightness around the soles of your feet, your ankles or your toes...

Draw in the healing energies of the <u>Plantain Golden Light Essence</u> and the beauty of Venus through your feet into your body; up into your heart and crown of the head.

Feel any pain dissolving. Focus on this process for a while.........

Have you been waiting for something you wish to manifest in your life? Let it come into your awareness now....

Focus intently on this wish.....See your feet taking you towards the manifestation and realisation of this wish.....See yourself fulfilling and attaining this wish.........Feel the joy, the bliss of having this very dear, personal wish granted.

Stay with this feeling for a while....

We thank Venus and <u>Plantain Golden Light Essence</u> for their healing energies.

Slowly become aware of your physical body again. Seal your aura with a cross of light in a circle of light for protection.

Come back to the room again and gently open your eyes.

You may want to contemplate your experience for a while.

27. RED CLOVER GOLDEN LIGHT ESSENCE
Guided Healing Meditation. (see Meditation CD).

Relax as you let go any tensions of mind or body......

Connect with your breath...

Let yourself be breathed naturally......

We call in the Deity Rowan, the element of Air, the energy of the planet Mercury, and the <u>Red Clover Golden Light Essence.</u>

Please be with us now....... Feel their presence.......

Bring us healing.........

Cleanse our lymph and blood of any impurities.

Bring us peace and calm and hope for spiritual, emotional and physical transformation and renewal.

Cleanse and disintegrate any negative thought forms in the base, heart and crown chakras with your healing white light.

Protect us from any negative energy in the lower astral realms and raise us in cosmic consciousness to the celestial, heavenly realms of healing white/golden Christ light.

Let this light illumine our hearts to pervade our whole being.......

Meditate on this process for a while....................

Thank you to our healers and to the red clover...

Gently become aware again of your physical body, the room around you and the flow of your breath... when you are ready, open your eyes......You may like to reflect on your experience...

28. ROSEMARY GOLDEN LIGHT ESSENCE
Guided Healing Meditation. (see Meditation CD).

Relax and let go of the cares of the day....

Focus on the breath....

We call in the energy of the moon, the Divine Mother and Saturn......
Be with us now......

We call in the rosemary plant for healing.....Be with us now.... Feel
their presence with you......

Focus on the heart area...... Go into the heart chakra.......

See the divine flame in your own heart and sit peacefully with this
flame/light for a while......

Feel the nurturing and healing energies as they uplift you......Stay
with this process for a while........Focus your attention on the crown
chakra.......See a pool of milk like a dish in the top of your head.
We ask the moon goddess to cleanse this pool, until it is pure white
and calm.Feel your mind becoming clearer and more peaceful.

Feel your mind and heart connecting and balancing your thoughts
and emotions.......Stay with this for a while....

Gently bring your awareness back to your physical body....

We thank the moon, the Divine Mother, healing Saturn and the
rosemary plant for any healing we have been able to receive.

When you are ready, open your eyes. You may like to contemplate
your experience for a while.

29. SARSPARILLA GOLDEN LIGHT ESSENCE
Guided Healing Meditation. (see Meditation CD).

Relax, letting go and cares, worries and physical tension in your mind and body........

Focus on the breath....Exhale.......Inhale.......

Continue breathing like this for a while......

Feel the stillness in the mind and body....

We call in the masculine, fire energy of mighty Jupiter as we travel to the sunny island of Jamaica.

The fire energy is strong but it does not burn us. The slightly cooling energy of the Sarsparilla vine and root washes over us, cleansing our minds of any negative thoughts and emotions...... cleansing the liver.........cleansing and balancing kidneys and adrenals......cleansing and balancing thyroid.........parathyroids... metabolism....reproductive hormones and organs, endocrine actions of the pancreas and blood sugars......easing any tension or heat in the nervous system....

Meditate on this balancing and cleansing action for a while.......

Feel any changes that may be taking place for you.........

Thank you Jupiter and Sarsparilla.......

Gently bring your awareness back to your body, the room and your surroundings.....

Open your eyes. Sit for a while to adjust to any new awareness you may feel ....

30. Skullcap Golden Light Essence
Guided Healing Meditation. (see Meditation CD).

Feel your body relaxing......Centre your attention on the breath..........

We call in the energy of the skullcap and the planet Saturn. We call in the Golden Angels of Healing of the 5 ELEMENTS….. Be with us now. Let us feel your presence......

Benevolent Saturn, please bring in your mighty life mastery healing and teaching energies to ground our restless minds and to bring peace and harmony to our emotions, adrenals and nervous system.

Feel the calm, steady, grounding energy pouring in at the pineal gland in the crown chakra........................

Stay with this calming and energizing feeling for a while...........

Focus on the breath to release any negativity ....

Breathe out negativity..........Breathe in positivity............

Feel the protection of the hooded blue skullcap flower all around you, especially in the head area and around the heart. Feel the protection of mighty Saturn.........Stay with these feelings and experiences for a while.......

Thank you skullcap. Thanks to you too mighty Saturn and thanks to the Golden Angels of Healing. In full faith. So be it and so it is.

Gently return your awareness to your physical body, to the room and to your surroundings.......

When you are ready, open your eyes.......breathe in an out….

You may want to contemplate your experiences for a while.

31. SUNFLOWER GOLDEN LIGHT ESSENCE
Guided Healing Meditation. (see Meditation CD).

Relax and focus on the breath for a while..............

We call upon the energy of the sunflower to bring balance to our solar plexus and heart chakras. We call upon the devic order of the Kachinas and the Vedas to bring higher wisdom and to temper the sun energy and the great Agni within and without. Let the sun warm but not burn us. Let the sun shine down divine wisdom upon us all in a way that we can receive this wisdom safely and effectively.

Let us increase our positive understanding of the Fathering aspect within our psyche. Let our hearts be cleansed and the feelings of sensitivity and caring be amplified. Let us feel the great protection of the sun. Let all the subtle bodies be aligned so that we will know if our intuitions and perceptions are accurate. Ease the idle chatter of the mind. Align the spinal energies and ease any strains in the spinal column, poor posture or spinal degeneration. Ease any sunburn or effects of sunburn. Dissolve any unwanted fatty tissue in our physical body. Let us have the awareness that All is One and One is All.

Bring a new awakening to our solar plexus chakra and heal, cleanse, balance and protect this chakra.

Thank you with great love and respect.........

Slowly and gently bring your awareness back to your physical body and to the room.... Breathe gently in and out........

Contemplate any new awareness you may have received......

32. VALERIAN GOLDEN LIGHT ESSENCE
Guided Healing Meditation. (see Meditation CD).

Relax and let go the tensions of the day.

Breathe out long.…..

Breathe in……. Focus on the breath for a while.…..

We call in the mighty St..George of England, slayer of dragons, transformer of the wild emotions of anger into tranquillity of spirit, peace and calm…….

Be with us now.…..

Feel St. George's presence.…..

We call in the healing spirit of the valerian plant.…..

Calm our spirits, emotions and nerves…….

Help us to release any tension in our nerves and muscles….

Clear our liver, solar plexus and heart from the heat of the emotion of anger bringing the soothing, cooling balm of peace.

Meditate on this peace for a while………

Thank you St. George and valerian for the healing we have been able to receive.

Bring your attention back to your physical body, the room, and when you are ready, open your eyes.

Stretch a little and if you like you can contemplate or write about your healing valerian experience.

33. Vervain Golden Light Essence
Guided Healing Meditation. (see Meditation CD).

I, <u>Vervain Golden Light Essence</u>, magically purify mind, body and soul, offering Divine protection from all harm.....

We travel to Stonehenge, the sacred site of the Druids. It is evening time and the sun is just setting. The star Sirius is rising. We sit here in this sacred Celtic site, surrounded by flowering, purple/blue Vervain plants.

Five Druid priests appear, wearing flowing white robes and holding silver sickles with which to harvest the Vervain plants. They cut the Vervain carefully, one by one, offering prayers and gifts of honey as thanks. We observe all of this closely..........

They sit and weave garlands from the Vervain plants and start to move towards us saying......"We the Druid high priests offer you a crown of Vervain...Wear this Vervain crown. It will protect you from all harm, all negative thoughts and greatly ease any nervous distress, giving you the gift of devotion, peace, calm and resilient nerves. It will help you to align yourself with God's will, so that you may walk the middle path and connect with the abundance of life which is your true birthright. It will help ground any new awakenings you may have and allow the continuous flow of Divine Grace in your lives. Blessings be to you dear ones....."

The Druid high Priests place the crown of vervain on your head and you feel very, very relaxed....

Meditate on this for a while...

We thank the Druid priests and watch as they quietly move away, blending into the large, stone pillars of Stonehenge. A crescent moon rises in the sky on this magical night of healing. Gently bring your awareness back to the room and your physical body.... When you are ready, open your eyes and stretch for a while. You may want to journal your experience.

34. VIOLET GOLDEN LIGHT ESSENCE
Guided Healing Meditation. (see Meditation CD).

Let your body and mind release any tension and feel sweet relaxation flow over you........

e call in the healing energy of Venus, the ancient Greek healers, Hippocrates and Pliny and the sweet violet plant....

Be with us now....Feel their Presence.........

We ask for your soothing and healing......

Cleanse our lymph of any harmful emotions, anger, trauma, anxiety and bring us sweet respite and true humility. Bring us true beauty and give us the ability to assert our true loving nature in the world and with others. Ease any spasms, tensions, sadness and over-excitement. Give strength to our heart muscles and give us true compassion. Calm, heal and cleanse our third eye chakra......Free us from all anxieties......

Bathe us in the healing energy of the <u>Violet Golden Light Essence</u>.

Stay with this soothing, healing energy for a while........

Gently bring your awareness back to the room. ....

We thank Venus, the Greek healers and the sweet violet plant for bringing us healing and protection......

When you are ready, gently open your eyes.

35. YARROW GOLDEN LIGHT ESSENCE
Guided Healing Meditation. (see Meditation CD).

Relax and let go of the cares of the day....... Focus your attention on the breath...........drop into your heart region.....

We call on the help of His Holiness the Dalai Lama, on the Tibetan Blue Medicine Buddha and the Deity White Tara....

Be with us now ...... Feel their presence....

We also invoke the Yarrow plant and all its healing qualities.... Be with us now dear Yarrow....We ask that our blood may be cleansed of all physical, emotional and psychic toxins and impurities....... We ask that these toxins be taken to the light for transmutation into positive, life enhancing energies. We ask that any wounds of the heart that we may have caused to others or that we have suffered ourselves be embalmed with the healing powers of the Yarrow plant and the compassion of White Tara........come to us dear Yarrow and White Tara......heal our hearts and lead us back to the Great Self of All........

Protect us from all negativity, pain, suffering and sorrow. Stay with this process for a while....

When you are ready, gently bring your attention to the room again and open your eyes.

We thank the Yarrow, the Dalai Lama and White Tara for this healing. You may want to contemplate your experience....

(This meditation was inspired by His Holiness the Dalai Lama after I attended His White Tara Puja and Initiation in Geelong, Australia on His visit here a few years ago. I thank my former student, friend and fellow Siddha Yogi Cleon Walters for taking me there.)

36. YELLOW DOCK GOLDEN LIGHT ESSENCE
Guided Healing Meditation. (see Meditation CD).

Breathe out…………..let the in breath arise naturally…..Let the out breath release naturally……….

Do this a few times…….Relax your body and mind…..feel easy…….

Focus your attention on the solar plexus area around the stomach and navel.

We call in the yellow dock and the planet Jupiter to expand our awareness of love and light and balance the *agni* – the fire energy- at the solar plexus.

We release all the dross, soot and ash which may have collected here along with the emotions of anger, rancour, sadness and any ill will we may have towards ourselves or others.

Let your body release these feelings and energies to the great fire – the *agni* – for purification and transformation into good will – Divine will.

Centre your attention on any unfulfilled heart-felt desire that you may have for yourself or others…..

"Mighty Jupiter, the magical yellow dock, we implore you to grant us the fulfilment of this heartfelt desire. May we be uplifted by grace and also contribute to the upliftment of those we love and others we many come into contact with during our everyday activities. May we remain humble and patient. May we be content." Thank you with great love……..

Stay with this state for a while…

Gently come back to the room…You may want to contemplate your experience for a while.

I hope you enjoy these meditations on the Golden Light Essences. Each week in 2009, as we meditated on one of these essences, profound healings and awakenings happened and we found ourselves enveloped and nurtured with our own golden divine light as it was freed more and more from its prison within to the outer reality of life in this dimension of time and space. An alchemy took place. A personal transmutation of the "lead" of our elements, into the "gold" of our true self started as this purification process unfolded. We reclaimed so much joy and love of life. So many nature Devis, planetary Angels, ancient healers and other helpful energies appeared to assist us in this journey of transformation. We gained a very intimate insight into the plants themselves as they whispered their healing secrets to us. The 5 Golden Light Angels of the Elements of fire, earth, water, air and ether were also with us.

I hope to have the meditation CD out for you very soon so that you can enjoy these meditations and the powerful healing experience they can bring to you, more deeply.

Chapter 8.   Living in the Golden Light

Seven years have passed since I experienced the awakening of the Golden Light. Since that time I have connected more and more with the Angelic Healing Kingdom and the 5 Golden Angels of the Elements and Karma who have shown me and my clients many paths of healing. Each month I conduct a healing Angel Meditation at my Golden Light Healing Clinic in Palmerston, Canberra. These healing evenings are truly a blessed event. The Angels continue to grace us with their Divine Presence and healing. I continue to give workshops on attuning people to this Golden Light Energy and using the Golden Light Essences for healing. My world of healing has expanded to include psychic healing mediumship, pranic healing and spiritual healing. The world of Spirit has opened up before me and continues to do so in many unexpected ways every day. I have days when feelings of happiness and bliss wash over me quite unexpectedly and spontaneously. The Golden Light keeps expanding and seems to have no limit in finding solutions to life's seeming 'problems'. I find myself here writing about it all and even re-experiencing the experiences as I do so. I have been giving public talks which often include guided meditations recently. These have started some powerful healing experiences for some people. I continue to use the essences in my Golden Light Healing Clinic and my clients love them.

My connection with the Plant Kingdom of Mother Earth continues as I make the Golden Light plant essences and discover deeper and deeper meaning and knowledge of their healing powers. I add the essences to patient's mixtures, use them on chakra points in spiritual healings and observe the profound transformations that take place. Mother Earth often gives me messages of thanks for doing this work of blessing the plant kingdom and raising its consciousness and the consciousness of humanity in this process. It is indeed a great Divine Alchemy of Transformation into grounding and blending the fifth dimension into this third dimension here on Earth.

For the last four years I have been conducting Angel Healing meditation evenings every month in my Golden Light Healing Clinic in which we have witnessed amazing personal and earth/planetary/cosmic healing. On Wednesday, the 6th February, 2008 which was Ash Wednesday with a partial lunar eclipse of the new moon in Aquarius, I felt guided to call in the five Golden Light Angels of Karma healing. During the preparation for that evening, the five Lords of Karma (beautiful Golden Light Beings who now accompany me everywhere as the five Golden Angels of Healing of the Elements and Karma) appeared to me, giving me instructions on how to proceed. I would like to share this with you now if you wish to heal some of your Karma effortlessly, with intent and surrender to your own great inner Golden Light. The message of the Karma Angels was "JUST FORGET IT"! This seemed a little banal at first, but later we realised what a profound message this was. We also remembered that where your attention goes, energy flows... so this message made a lot of sense to us at the meditation.

You can prepare yourself as you would for meditation and then call in the Five Golden Angels, Lords of Karma as follows:

Be with me now Angels /Lords of Karma. Let me feel your Presence with me now. Feel their Presence.

You may like to ask, "May I have karmic release from _____ (my illness, life situation, problem, relationship, work situation etc.)? Make your request very clear and simple. Or you may like to ask, "May I have complete karmic healing for my relationship with _____ (name the person, living or not.)?

Feel, hear or intuit the response as Yes/No. Ask the Angels/Lords of Karma for a clear response or ask, "May I/we have this healing through all the levels, all the bodies and all the lifetimes, including the present lifetime. Please heal all the damage from this relationship/situation/ illness or problem and bring the healing into the present NOW. Thank you with great love and respect.

If your answer was NO, ask the Lords/Angels of Karma…"what do I need to know to have this healing?"

Don't argue with the Angels of Karma, just ask for new understanding at this time or at the appropriate time. Let go of any expectations or ask, "What can I do to heal or release this?" Then affirm for as long as you feel you need to each day… ANGELS of KARMA , HELP ME WITH RIGHT ACTION TODAY. Thank you. Observe what happens over the next few weeks and months. You can repeat this process for any other issues you would like to release and have healed. You may also like to take some of the appropriate <u>GOLDEN LIGHT ESSENCES</u> *to help you peel back the emotions surrounding the matter. Please refer to the chapter on how to use the essences, especially for Karmic healing.*

On the night of this powerful encounter and healing with the five Golden Angels of Karma, I had a very personal experience of their beautiful healing energies. I awoke in the middle of the night from my sleep, to see my bedroom glowing in bright golden light and a vision of the five Golden Angels/Lords of Karma appeared before me. They showed me my Golden Book of Life with my name on it and burnt it up in flames in front of me. Then the last page of my Golden Book of Life appeared with my name Pati-pat Shiva (my spiritual name) on it and the message in flaming letters of gold "You are a divine golden light being Pati-pat Shiva." Then they departed, leaving me shaking but incredibly peaceful and feeling very, very blessed. I thanked them and soon fell asleep. For the next few days, I felt rather 'floaty' and the Golden Light was very strong in me and around me. I am still trying to make sense of what happened that night. I feel it was a great blessing. You never know what might happen when you connect with this Golden Light Energy and the five Golden Angels of Healing. One thing I do know, is that it is all good and that these beings are fair and love us so much. They can appear fierce and sometimes gentle but at all times must be treated with the greatest reverence, respect and of course great love and surrender to Spirit.

Over the last few years, I have had repeated visitation from these Divine Beings in meditation, in my personal and client healing and in messages of help which they continue to send me every day. They have asked me to write about my experiences with them. They bring me psychic messages of healing for others. I have developed a very close bond with these Golden Angels. This has enhanced my life in every possible way. I know that they give me what I need for my highest good. This is not necessarily what I might always want. They surround me with great protection and strength. I have seen this happen for others too.

If you feel guided by Spirit to do so, you can call them in anytime for help and protection and healing by simply asking, "Golden Angels of the five Elements and Karma, be with me now. Thank you. And so it is."

They will assist you in every way in moving into the fifth dimension of living here on Mother Earth at this time, bring you great beauty, abundance, well being, good health and much, much more. Above all they will bring you closer and closer to the realization of who YOU really are and who we all are in truth - Golden Divine Beings of Light and Love in a human body, living at this time on Mother Earth to just experience life, growing in consciousness and awareness of the joy of life.

Recently, I have had some new insights about healing and the Golden Light Body. Healing is about letting go and releasing, releasing, releasing all that we think we are into the All that we really are - the great Divine Golden Light which pervades everything and everyone. This is the Divine cosmic energy which we feel as the Spirit or Life Force within us. When we are able surrender more and more to this Golden Light we become relaxed at deeper levels, easing any physical tension and experiencing more of the Golden Light Body right here in this physical life. As this happens we start to experience all of life as being interconnected and ourselves as part of this All, this connectedness. As a result we find our lives flowing more easily no matter what might be happening externally. If we are ill or in pain, help comes in the form of situations and people who can assist us. We live more and more in harmony with the flow of life. Our suffering lessens whatever our personal life circumstances may be. I leave you today with the words of my favourite wise woman and mystic from the middle ages

"Holy Spirit…you are our true life, luminous, wonderful, awakening the heart from its ancient sleep."

-Hildegard of Bingen

Appendix A: Some Common Ailments and Indications for use of the Essences.

Here are some common ailments and the indications for the use of the 36 Golden Light Essences for healing:

Accidents/Trauma	*Yarrow*
Aches	*Comfrey*
Acne	*Burdock*
Addictions	*Iris*
Adrenals	*Sarsparilla/Hops*
Allergies	*Alfalfa*
Amenorrhoea	*Peony*
Anemia	*Damask Rose*
Anorexia	*Gentian*
Anxiety	*Violet Leaf*
Arteries	*Elderflower*
Arthritis	*Meadowsweet*
Asthma	*Hyssop*
Aura broken	*Mugwort*
Aura misaligned	*Lotus*
Back Pain (general)	*Skullcap*
Balance	*Plantain*
Baldness	*Rosemary*
Bedwetting	*Hypericum*
Bite/insects	*Alfalfa*
Blisters	*Golden Seal*
Blood disorders	*Meadowsweet*

Blood Pressure Balance	*Lemon Balm*
Body odour	*Fenugreek*
Boils	*Burdock*
Bone fracture	*Comfrey*
Bone Marrow	*Yarrow/Comfrey*
Brain imbalances	*Lotus*
Breasts	*Violet Leaf/Fenugreek*
Bronchitis	*Elderflower/Hyssop*
Bruising	*Comfrey/Damask Rose*
Bulimia	*Gentian*
Burns	*Sunflower*
Car sickness	*Lavender*
Cataracts	*Burdock*
Cholesterol Imbalance	*Fenugreek/Ginger*
Circulation	*Mistletoe/Damask Rose*
Colds	*Mugwort/Ginger*
Colic	*Chamomile*
Colitis	*Mary's Thistle*
Conjunctivitis	*Damask Rose*
Constipation	*Yellow Dock*
Coughs	*Plantain/Hyssop/Elderflowers*
Cramps (muscle)	*Valerian*
Cuts	*Golden Seal*
Cystitis	*Plantain/Lemon Balm*
Cysts	*Red Clover/Violet Leaf*
Deafness	*Plantain*
Depression	*Lemon Balm*
Diarrhoea	*Mary's thistle*
Dizziness	*Lotus*
Ear problems	*Plantain/Lavender*
Eczema	*Hypericum/Alfalfa*
Eyes	*Iris/Gardenia*
3rd eye	*Gardenia*

Fatigue	*Sunflower*
Fever	*Passionflower/Vervain/Elderflower*
Food Poisoning	*Mugwort/Golden Seal*
Foot Problems	*Plantain*
Frustration	*Iris*
Gallstones	*Gentian/Yellow Dock*
Gout	*Lavender*
Gum problems	*Golden Seal*
Haemorrhoids	*Mary's Thistle*
Heart	*Damask rose/Gardenia*
Herpes	*Lavender/Lemon Balm*
Hives	*Alfalfa*
Hyperactivity	*Chamomile*
High/Low Blood Sugar	*Iris*
Impotence	*Peony*
Incontinence	*Plantain*
Indigestion	*Chamomile/Alfalfa/Meadowsweet*
Infection	*Golden Seal*
Insanity	*Peony/Lotus/Gardenia*
Infertility	*Fenugreek*
Influenza	*Elderflower*
Insomnia	*Mugwort/Passionflower/Lemon Balm*
Itching	*Alfalfa/Chamomile*
Jaw problems	*Valerian*
Jet Lag	*Hypericum/Alfalfa*
Kidney problems	*Lavender/Lemon Balm/Vervain*
Knee problems	*Comfrey*
Laryngitis	*Kelp*
Liver disorders	*Yellow Dock/Valerian/Mary's Thistle*
Lung problems	*Hyssop/Elderflowers/Hypericum*
Maleria	*Mugwort/Mary's Thistle*
Memory	*Rosemary/Lotus*
Menopause	*Sarsparilla*

Menstrual problems	*Peony*
Muscles	*Oats*
Nails	*Comfrey*
Nausea	*Iris/Mary's thistle*
Neck	*Yarrow/Mugwort*
Nervous problems	*Hops/Vervain/Alfalfa*
Nosebleeds	*Yarrow*
Ovaries	*Red Clover/Sarsparilla/Peony*
Overweight	*Fenugreek/Meadowsweet*
Pain general	*Hypericum*
Pancreas	*Iris/Golden Seal*
Paralysis	*Oats/Mistletoe*
Parasites	*Mistletoe/Mugwort/Yellow Dock*
Pineal Gland	*Hypericum*
PMT	*Peony*
Prostate	*Peony/Oats/Fenugreek*
Psoriasis	*Oats/Alfalfa/Burdock*
Radiation	*Yarrow*
Rheumatism	*Yellow Dock*
Sciatica	*Burdock*
Senility	*Plantain/Lotus*
Shock	*Yarrow*
Sinusitis	*Elderflowers/Alfalfa/Fenugreek*
Smoking quitting	*Plantain*
Snoring	*Hyssop/Mugwort*
Spleen	*Mistletoe/Red Clover*
Stiffness	*Comfrey*
Stroke	*Lemon Balm*
Sunburn	*Sunflower*
Teeth	*Comfrey/Plantain*
Testicles problems	*Peony/Violet Leaf/Sarsparilla*
Throat problems	*Kelp*
Thyroid	*Iris/Kelp*

Tiredness	*Alfalfa*
Toxicity	*Yarrow*
Uterus	*Rosemary/Peony*
Varicose Veins	*Mary's Thistle/Yellow Dock*

Appendix B: A simple explanation of some of the Ayurvedic terms used

Ayurveda is the system of medicine and healing developed by the great Vedic/Yogic sages and is still used today. It has been used in India for ages and is finding great popularity in other countries. The underlying philosophy of this healing system is to restore the constitutional health of your basic type (Dosha). There are three basic doshas: Pitta, Kapha and Vata or any combination of these:

> Pitta contains more of the elements of fire and water.
> Kapha contains more of the elements of water and earth.
> Vata contains more of the elements of air and ether.

The understanding is that we are all made up of these 5 elements in some combination and that this is our Prakruti or constitutional type. The more we are in balance with our Prakruti, the more we experience good health and wellbeing and also progress on the spiritual path we have chosen in this lifetime.

According to this philosophy of life there are also three Gunas, prime attributes or basic qualities to all life. These are:
Sattva: the principle of light, perception, intelligence, love and harmony.
Rajas: the principle of energy, activity, emotion and turbulence.
Tamas: the principle of inertia, darkness, dullness and resistance.
All three qualities are necessary in nature, but individuals in whom sattva predominates, give value to truth, honesty, humility and the good of all.

The prana or life force pervading all of creation, all the nadis (energy channels) and chakras (energy receivers) of the human body, can be used to keep us in balance. As the doshas go out of balance by "ignorance of our true nature", or the "wrong understanding "of a life situation, toxins or ama can accumulated in the tissues and cause disease. When we release this "ama", health and wellbeing return.

Ayurvedic philosophy also recognises that we are part of the greater universe and planetary energies and so sees all of life as intimately linked to the plants, planets and all of creation. This is where the Vedic system of astrology comes in. Ayurveda is a complex system of healing and this explanation only touches the surface. There are many good texts on Ayurveda if you would like to learn more.

Resources

1. Dr. David Frawley & Dr.Vasant Lad: **The Yoga of Herbs** (Lotus Press, Wisconsin, U.S.A.1988.)

2. Dr.RajenCooppan: **Foundation & Advanced Training in Clinical Ayurveda** course, 2000/2001/2002. Manual and notes of course.

3. Jeffrey Armstrong: **Vedic Astrology Deck and Guide.** (Mandala publishing, U.S.A., 2005)

4. Swami Shantananda: **The Splendor of Recognition,** An exploration of the *Pratyabhijna-hrdayam.* A text on the Ancient Science of the Soul. (A Siddha Yoga Publication, South Fallsburg, N.Y., U.S.A., 2003)

5. Julianne Bien: **Golden Light** – A journey with Advanced Colorworks. (Spectrahue light & sound inc., Toronto, Canada.)

6. Chok C. Hiew: **Tao of Healing** – The Incredible Golden Light Energy (iUniverse.com.Inc., U.S.A. 2000).

7. Patricia Mercier: **Chakras.** Balance your Body's Energy for Health and Harmony. (Sterling Publishing Co. Inc., New York, 2000).

8. Hildegard of Bingen: **Illuminations of Hildegard of Bingen** (with commentary by Matthew Fox.) Bear & Company, Santa Fee, New Mexico, 1985

9. Jennifer Edwards: **The Golden Light**. *Love, Life and Your Spiritual Purpose* (Athena Press, London, 2007).

10. Gurudas: **Flower Essences and Vibrational Healing** (Cassandra Press, San Rafael, CA, 1989).

Acknowledgments

I would like to thank all the people who made this book possible. My patients and students who trusted me with their personal healing and especially to those who contributed their healing experiences to the book, I thank you profoundly. I would like to thank Kim Knight who edited much of this book and came up with a marketing plan for this project. To Angie and Jim Matsinos, for the artwork of the cover and the 36 Golden Light Essence divinatory card pack, a big thank you. I also thank my daughter Luci Knight for her patience and help in educating her Mum in computing. To my husband, Klaus Hueneke, I thank you for supporting me both emotionally and financially in the production of this book and for creating the beautiful garden from which many of the essences come. For all the inspiration I received from the five Golden Angels of Healing, I thank you with all my heart. I feel your Presence with me constantly.

With great love and thanks to all the others whom I have not mentioned personally, but who know who they are in spirit.
Pati Solva Hueneke

Canberra/Australia, 17th of August, 2010.